MW00910635

Charlie King
We called him "Blackie"

by Bobby J. Copeland

Published by:

Empire Publishing, Inc.
P. O. Box 717
Madison, NC 27025-0717

Phone: 336-427-5850 • Fax: 336-427-7372
Email: movietv@pop.vnet.net

Other books by Bobby J. Copeland:
Trail Talk, published by Empire Publishing, Inc.
B-Western Boot Hill, by Empire Publishing, Inc.
Bill Elliott – The Peaceable Man, by Empire Publishing, Inc.
Roy Barcroft – King of the Badmen, by Empire Publishing, Inc.
Silent Hoofbeats, by Empire Publishing, Inc.
The Whip Wilson Story, self-published
The Bob Baker Story, self-published
Five Heroes, self-published

Empire Publishing, Inc.
PO Box 717
Madison, NC 27025-0717
Phone: 336-427-5850
Fax: 336-427-7372
Email: movietv@pop.vnet.net

Charlie King—We Called Him Blackie copyright © 2003 by Bobby J. Copeland

All rights reserved under International and Pan American copyright convention. No part of this book may be reproduced in any manner whatsoever without written permission from the publisher, except in the case of brief quotations embodied in reviews and articles.

Library of Congress Control Number: 2002116142
ISBN Number: 0-944019-40-4

Published and printed in the United States of America
1 2 3 4 5 6 7 8 9 10

COVER ARTWORK by Bobb Lynes

CONTENTS

DEDICATION

Dedicated to:

Les Adams and Chuck Anderson …
Whose major contributions made this work possible.

And, to Neil Summers … who is always willing to share his
vast collection of photographs for my projects.

ACKNOWLEDGMENTS
and Selected Bibliographies

Western Clippings published by Boyd Magers
Wrangler's Roost published by Colin Momber
Those Great Cowboy Sidekicks by David Rothel
Hollywood Corral by Don Miller
Saturday Afternoon at the Movies by Alan G. Barbour
Cliffhanger by Alan G. Barbour
Trail Talk by Bobby J. Copeland
The Filming of the West by Jon Tuska
Tex Ritter – America's Most Beloved Cowboy by Bill O'Neal
The Badmen I Rode With by Pierce Lyden
Battlin' Bob Steele by Mario DeMarco
Wrangler's Roost article by John Brooker
A Job for Superman by Kirk Alyn

Les Adams
Bill McDowell
Richard B. Smith III
Chuck Anderson
Boyd Magers
Grady Franklin
William C. Russell
Paul Dellinger
Kenneth Kitchen
John Leonard
Tinsley Yarbrough

Bobb Lynes
George Coan
Ken Jones
Bill Sasser
Jim Hamby
Joe Copeland
Lance Copeland
Ralph Absher
Neil Summers
Rhonda Lemons
Doneen Key

CHARLIE KING — We called him "Blackie"

"There's Old Blackie; he's a crook," the front row kids would yell every time the rotund, mustached man with the evil look appeared on the Saturday matinee movie screen. As kids we didn't know his name, but we later found out it was Charles King.

If there is one actor, other than perhaps Roy Barcroft, who epitomized the bad guy of the B-Western, it has to be Charlie King. He could ride, shoot, and fight with the best of them. When he mixed it up with the hero, he put on such a good show it was always exciting and a delight to witness. He was truly a professional, and he was an outstanding character actor who could portray a comic, sidekick, boss heavy, lawman, or just an ordinary gang member. Whatever the role, he delivered a fine performance.

King must be considered the best of the villains during the '30s and the early '40s, just as Roy Barcroft was the best from the mid-'40s until the demise of B-Westerns. Some fans are divided on which one was the best. They both were great. Charles King's fights with Bob Steele are considered classics just as Barcroft's fights with Allan "Rocky" Lane. Charlie had a career that spanned from the silents, and was a menace to almost every B-Western cowboy.

Trying to find information on King was a most difficult task.

Although he was well liked by his peers, it seems he had his own inner circle of friends (probably his drinking buddies), and did not socialize much outside of that circle or grant interviews. We do know his father was a physician; Charlie was married and divorced; a hard worker, a collector of rare firearms, an alcoholic, and most reports said he fathered three sons.

It's too bad much more wasn't written about King's personal life. Of course, the press was usually only interested in the leading men, and had little concern for the character actors. Perhaps Don Miller, in his book *Hollywood Corral*, said it best: "It was the star that counted; nobody ever remembered the names of the characters in B movies." However, noted Western film historian William K. Everson had a deep appreciation for the character actors and for King in particular. Everson, in dedicating his book, *The Bad Guys*, to Charlie wrote, "To Charles King who was THE badman to all of us who bounced up and down on our seats at the Saturday matinees throughout the thirties an forties."

Although reports say King had only three sons, veteran researcher Les Adams says King had a daughter named Patricia. Mr. Adams goes on to say, "She was married to Eddie Hall for a short time. Which is probably the reason Eddie Hall is in the 1945 PRC Buster Crabbe film, SHADOWS OF DEATH. Perhaps King's influence got his new son-in-law a part in the movie."

(Hall's performance must have not been impressive, or maybe it was because the marriage was on the rocks and King no longer intervened on Hall's behalf, but, for whatever reason, he made few screen appearances.)

Apparently, King started working in Hollywood before the 1920s. And when sound arrived, he really came into his own as a Western villain. He appeared in productions from Universal, Columbia, Monogram, and Republic, as well as lower-budget stuff from companies such as Tiffany, Colony, KBS World Wide, PRC, and more. His deep growl of a voice and heavyset physique made him a natural for his roles as a villain. He could

Buster Crabbe, Eddie Hall, King and Al St. John

also handle himself on horseback, and was a real pro in the fights. Off screen, Charlie was known for his rowdy sense of humor, which caused him to be big favorite with his peers.

It seemed that in almost every film you looked at in the '30s there would be Old Charlie getting beaten up by Bob Steele, Hoot Gibson, Buck Jones, Tex Ritter, or some other defender of justice. He'd be knocked over chairs, tables, bars, or stairs at the mere drop of a hat.

King's work must have been quite competent because it was not limited to Westerns. He can also be spotted doing bit parts in B-melodramas, crime flicks, serials, et. al, where he appeared as a member of a gang, or a driver, or whatever role he could find.

Although King worked with almost all the sound Western stars, it is his bouts with Bob Steele and Tex Ritter that are the best remembered. His encounters with them were long and often.

Mario DeMarco wrote in his book, *Battlin' Bob Steele*, about Charlie's ability in his battles with Steele: "I can only number one hero that could match "Blackie's" skill with his dukes, and that was Bob Steele. Second to Bob would be Tex Ritter. Steele, a one-time boxer (he did some boxing as an amateur. Despite many reports, according to his brother Jim, he did not box professionally), would first go over the fight scenes carefully with Charlie. The timing became perfect. When Bob would jab his left three or four times in quick succession, King's head would jerk back so realistic that the audience thought he was actually getting pulverized. Then Bob would finish him off with a left and a right cross that usually sent King sprawling across a table or two into a dead heap. Both were real experts in this particular scene. When Charlie took on a bit of weight in later years, it tended to make the thin, athletic Steele look twice as good."

Charlie has been bested once more by Battlin' Bob Steele (THE TRUSTED OUTLAW, Republic, 1937).

Perhaps Tex Ritter is telling Charlie, "This town's not big enough for both of us."

If King looked good with Steele, he was almost equally brilliant with Tex Ritter. Bill O'Neal wrote in *Tex Ritter – America's Most Beloved Cowboy,* "Tex was carefully tutored in handling his fists by an expert in screen brawls — Charlie King. Charlie had a thick build while Tex was tall and rangy. They looked good as opponents, and Tex demonstrated a knack for screen fisticuffs, which was choreographed by Charlie. The two men enjoyed staging brawls, and Tex rarely used a double. On screen, Charlie would pick a fight, Tex would quickly rise to the challenge, and fists and furniture would begin flying."

Ritter (1905) was a decade older than Charlie (1895), but the age difference did not hinder their fight scenes. Tex had great admiration for King's ability and said of him, "I was pretty tough (in the movies). Roy and Gene sang more — I killed more. I must have shot Charlie King a hundred times. Usually, it was behind the same rock. You've got to give Charlie King credit. He was a ballet artist the way he went about it. And he was a natural comedian. He was always so surly on the screen that very few people would have guessed his comic talent. He would occasionally give a spasmodic kick when knocked out to sort of accentuate the make-believe."

(Once, while on a date, Tex and his lady friend were robbed at gunpoint. Tex said of the incident, "I thought about fighting him, but he didn't look like Charlie King, and the bullets in his gun didn't look like blanks.")

It has been rumored that the battles between Steele and King were instrumental in the development of one of the greatest heavyweight boxing champions of the world — Joe Louis. Joe, as a youngster, became so inspired by watching these two mixing it up on the screen that he took up boxing — imitating his hero, Bob Steele.

It was also rumored that King was denied admission to the Motion Picture Home due to the type of films (low budget) he made. If he was denied admission, in all probability, it was due to his alcoholism rather than the type of films in which he appeared. Many other low-budget performers have been admitted to the Home.

Some of King's last work was in the "Texas Rangers" series, and with Buster Crabbe. In the "Texas Rangers" series, he was again reunited with one of his old slugfest opponents, Tex Ritter. King, by this time, had grown a large paunch. And he sometimes wore ragged clothes, a worn out hat, and even a Snub Pollard type mustache – the same type of attire usually worn by the cowboy sidekicks. In fact, Charlie looked much like a former Ritter sidekick — Horace Murphy — did in the movie TROUBLE IN TEXAS (Grand National, 1937). King was often involved with some of the comedy scenes, and, at times, he was much more funny than Guy Wilkerson, the man getting paid to be funny in the series. Although still one of the villains, Charlie's fights were now exercises in slapstick, and the films were not helped by the loss of his menace. But he did briefly knock out Dave O'Brien in DEAD OR ALIVE (PRC, 1944), giving him a momentary sense of superiority.

Some may have thought Charlie had gone on a diet and got back down to his ideal fighting weight when they viewed the 1950 Johnny Mack Brown Monogram movie, LAW OF THE PANHANDLE. Alas, this was not the case. They were seeing nine-year-old stock footage of Charlie taken from the "Rough Riders" picture FORBIDDEN TRAILS (Monogram, 1941), which had been inserted into the film.

Buster Crabbe fought King many times as did Crabbe's side-kick Fuzzy St. John. Crabbe discussed the battles between St. John and King: "I don't know how many times Fuzzy fought with Charlie King, but I do know they put on a hell of a battle in a lot of pictures. You know Charlie King started out as a comic,

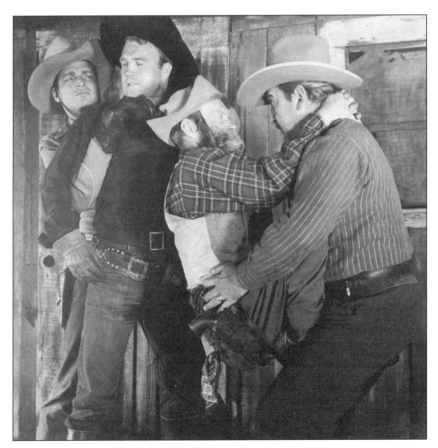

This time Buster has a headlock on John Cason while Charlie is in the grasp of Fuzzy St. John (PRAIRIE BADMEN, PRC, 1946).

but then they gave him a black hat, and he played a lot of heavies. Fuzzy and he would work out a routine between them for these comic fights – funny, really funny. And when something went wrong, it was even funnier – when one of them miscued on a tumble or something like that."

(In Crabbe's last starring Western, OUTLAWS OF THE PLAINS (PRC, 1946), it is Fuzzy, not Buster, who captures King by bulldogging him off his horse. Anyone who watches this film can plainly see it is really Fuzzy's film. In fact, Buster doesn't show up until about 15 minutes into the movie).

King did most of his work for these *directors*:

1. Sam Newfield (59 films)
2. Ray Taylor (21 films)
3. Harry Fraser (17 films)
4. Robert N. Bradbury (16 films)
5. Robert Tansey (13 films)
6. Spencer Gordon Bennet and Al Herman (12 films each)

King did most of his films with these *heroes*:

1. Bob Steele (29 films)
2. Buster Crabbe (24 films)
3. Tex Ritter (23 films)
4. Johnny Mack Brown (20 films)
5. Dave O'Brien in the "Texas Rangers" series (19 films)
6. Ken Maynard (17 films)
7. Buck Jones (16 films)

The above includes trio series — "Three Mesquiteers", "Texas Rangers", "Rough Riders", "Trail Blazer", etc.

King did most of his work at these *studios*:

1. Producers Releasing Corp. (PRC) - 75 films across eight years

2. Monogram - 57 films across 19 years
3. Columbia - 47 films across 23 years
4. Republic - 43 films across 14 years
6. Universal - 21 films across 13 years

King appeared in:

- 38 serials
- 19 of the 22 "Texas Rangers" films
- 6 of the 24 "Range Busters" films
- 5 of the 8 "Trail Blazers" films
- 5 of the 8 "Rough Riders' films"
- 4 of the 51 "Three Mesquiteers" films

You can run your own searches in King's filmography. But it's interesting to note that King did *NOT* appear in the following Western film series:

- William Boyd "Hopalong Cassidy" series
- Allan Lane series
- Monte Hale series
- Rex Allen series
- Bob Baker series
- The Dorothy Page "singing cowgirl" Westerns
- Whip Wilson series
- Reb Russell series
- Dick Foran series
- He made only one film with Sunset Carson, Tim Holt, Kirby Grant, and Rod Cameron, and two film appearances with Roy Rogers.
- He made only two films at RKO, one for Fox, and no films for Warners, Paramount, or United Artists.

King was also not spotted in the following cowboy series: Guinn "Big Boy" Williams, Bob Allen, James Warren, Jimmy Ellison/ Russell Hayden, The "Rough Riding Kids", and he was in none of the Cisco Kid films.

(It may surprise the reader to see that King appeared with Crabbe 24 times, one more time than he did with Tex Ritter. He worked with Bob Steele 29 times.)

Everyone knows Charlie became an alcoholic, but it was said it never affected his work. Although he appeared in pictures for many years, he spent freely, and was often in need of money.

He was known to "hit on" his friends for loans that they knew would never be repaid. Movie badman, Terry Frost said, "Charlie was a great guy, but he was an alcoholic. He tried to kill himself twice. One time, he shot himself with a .22, and another time he climbed a tree and tried to hang himself. Either the limb or the rope broke, and Charlie ended up with a broken leg. The last time I saw him, he said, 'Terry, can you help me out?' I gave him a five-spot. I knew I would never see it again, and that he was going to buy a bottle with it, but I thought, oh, what the hell."

(Frost, a long time co-worker and friend of King's, was also a heavy drinker, and he was living in rather poor conditions until he married a rich woman and former actress Marion Carney. After Frost's death, Lash LaRue moved in with Carney. She later became Mrs. LaRue number 12.)

Various sources mention King's wife as being very assertive, and she would often accompany him when he picked up his paycheck ... which she immediately confiscated to ensure that they had groceries in the house.

Why didn't Charlie King make any movies in 1951 and 1952? And why didn't he do more television after the demise of B-Westerns? This is

Terry Frost

a question posed by many Western film enthusiasts. Several of Charlie's peers did move on to the small screen, and made good contributions, including Bud Osborne, Tris Coffin, Terry Frost, Bob Cason, Kenne Duncan, I. Stanford Jolley, Jack Ingram, Dick Curtis, Kenneth MacDonald, George J. Lewis, Edmund Cobb, Lane Bradford, Holly Bane (also known as Michael Ragan), and many others, but not Charlie, who apparently appeared only in a few crowd scenes in "Gunsmoke".

Word did get around fast at the various studios during those days, and maybe they had been warned of King's drinking and no longer considered him reliable. Whatever the reason for Charlie's disappearance from the screen, we will never know.

Perhaps it was King's drinking and his extra weight, or his suicide attempts that caused an end to his screen career, and prevented him from going into TV. At any rate, he had to seek other employment. Jim Martin (a fan from Arizona wrote about an incident in the latter part of King's life): "About 1955 or '56, I went out to the San Fernando Valley to Menasco Steel Company, and had to check in at the security guard's office in the rear before I could get in. The security guard was Charlie King. He was working there to supplement his retirement after leaving the movie business, and continued working there until he died. We had quite a long conversation before I had to finish my business, and talked a few more times after that whenever I got back there."

If, indeed, it was Charlie's drinking that caused him seek employment outside the movie business, it seems strange that he would be hired as a security guard.

King's latter years were apparently anything but golden. It has been rumored that he ended up on skid row. This is entirely possible since we know he was an alcoholic, divorced, and hit upon his friends for loans. It is a shame, but it could very well be that this man with over 300 screen credits ended up as a bum.

Some have claimed King died of a heart attack immediately

after playing a corpse on the "Gunsmoke" TV show, but that is not the case. It was his drinking that did Charlie in. He died of cirrhosis of the liver and chronic alcoholism, not a heart attack. I think the reason the "Gunsmoke" story got started was because there was a technician on the program named Charles King. Many feel that it was he who played the corpse, and then died of a heart attack. When it was reported a Charles King had died, people only assumed it was Charles King the actor.

(Strangely enough, a similar story occurred about the "death" of King's number one screen nemesis, Bob Steele. In the 1960s, a man from Tennessee was going around claiming to be Bob Steele. When he died, it made the newspapers that the cowboy star Bob Steele had passed away. When Steele was informed, he was only amused. Everyone still has not realized the truth. Only recently (Spring of 2002), a lady called this writer saying she knew Bob Steele was from Rogersville, Tennessee, because her father used to run around with him. When I politely tried to correct her, she hung up the telephone on me.

You can bet Bob Steele has a plan to get the gun away from Charlie.

Western historians know Bob Steele was born in Portland, Oregon, grew up in California, and never resided in Tennessee.)

King worked in films under several variations of his name including Charles King and Charles King, Jr. Because he sometimes used the Jr., some writers have said that King's son worked in pictures. However, that is not the case as King and King, Jr., were one in the same. His film credits are often confused with the musical-comedy star with the same name. This Charles King starred in BROADWAY MELODY (MGM, 1929), among others. He died of pneumonia in 1944 while entertaining troops in England.

Buster Crabbe is ready to slug Black Jack O'Shea, while Fuzzy wallops Charlie with a bag.

WHERE ARE CHARLIE'S ASHES?

According to his death certificate, Charlie was pronounced dead at the John Wesley County Hospital in Los Angeles. He was cremated at the Grandview Crematory in Glendale, California. The ashes were then sent to a funeral home in Charlie's hometown, Hillsboro, Texas. However, the Texas funeral home has no record of receiving the ashes, so where are Charlie's ashes? Another mystery on the certificate is the fact that King's mother's name is listed as "unknown", even though the informant for the document was Charles S. King.

Who is Charles S. King? Some think he and Charles King III are one in the same. Perhaps he was a grandson.

The disappearance of King's ashes is reminiscent of the mystery surrounding the ashes of another cowboy hero who worked with Charlie — Lash LaRue. The following article by publisher Boyd Magers comes from the January/February 1997 issue of *Western Clippings*:

> "Lash LaRue's widow, Marion Carney Callahan Frost LaRue, is suing Forest Lawn Memorial Park, where Lash's body was taken after his May 21 (1996) death, claiming her husband's body was lost, or his ashes were mixed with others. I was aware of Marion's claims shortly after Lash's death, but elected not to report her accusations, as they could not be substantiated. Her story/ac-

cusations have varied slightly from telling to telling. When I spoke to Marion early last summer, she had variously reported Forest Lawn had lost Lash's body or lost his ashes or cremated him prematurely. She told me and others she'd gone to Forest Lawn within days or a week later (the lawsuit claims three days), to obtain a lock of Lash's hair, and was told they were unable to comply as he'd already been cremated. They apparently offered her an urn containing ashes, which she told me she refused, claiming it either wasn't Lash's, or the ashes were mixed with other remains. Many of you met Marion when she was married to the late Terry Frost, and attended various Western film festivals with him. I have only chosen to mention this somber story now because the Associated Press picked up the lawsuit from court records in late November, and brief stories have appeared in various newspapers. Sadly, until the suit is resolved, Lash's ashes will not see a final resting place."

When this writer was seeking information for my book *B-West-*

It's breakfast time with King, Fuzzy, and Lash (LAW OF THE LASH, PRC, 1947).

ern Boot Hill (1999), I learned that Lash's ashes were still un-
claimed and stored at Forest Lawn.)

Charlie King's death record

The California Death Records database lists Charles Lafayette
King; born 2/21/1895, in Texas; died 5/07/1957; Social Security number of 561-01-4156. Although he had a long and varied career, his death did not rate a single line in *Daily Variety,*
and only a few lines in *The Hollywood Reporter.*

- **Information from King's death certificate reads:**
  Name: Charles Lafayette King, Jr.
  Place of death: John Wesley County Hospital, Los Ange-
  les, CA
  Date of death: May 7, 1957. Hour: 7:45 p.m.
  Date of birth: Feb. 21, 1895
  Specify marriage: Divorced
  Usual occupation: Actor. Kind of business or industry:
  Motion picture studio
  Name and birthplace of father: Charles Lafayette King,
  Sr., Kentucky

- Maiden name and birthplace of mother: Unknown
  Birthplace: Texas
  Social Security No: 561-01-4156
  Informant: Charles S. King
  Armed forces: Yes, WWII
  Last usual address: 4914 Bellaire Avenue, North
  Hollwood, CA
  Cause of death: Hepatic coma
  Antecedent causes: Cirrhosis and chronic alcoholism
  Burial: Cremation

*(If Charlie was in WWII, it had to be brief because he made
many movies during this time frame. However, he was old
enough to have served in WWI.)*

A death certificate was also located for King's son Charles

Lafayette King, III. On this document we do learn the name of Charlie King's wife. It was Pauline Dorothy Nelson, and she was born in Arizona. We also learn that King, III, was murdered in 1990 (shot in the chest).

King, III, also worked in the movie business, as a mixer.

(Mix is the process by which separate sound tracks (dialogue, music, sound effects, etc.) are combined on a single sound track for eventual use in composite print. The process is carried out at a mixing console equipped with many control knobs and push buttons for balancing the various control elements. The sound technician who operates the mixing console is called a "mixer".)

This friendship can't last long. Hal Price, Don Barry, and King.

HOW MANY TIMES DID CHARLIE PLAY BLACKIE?

(Author's Note: veteran researcher Les Adams contributes the following. I think the reader is in for a big surprise.)

Well, finding the answer to that brought up other questions as I followed the search-and-find process through my database on this fine new piece of Dell (Texas-based, of course) equipment that is faster than a speeding bullet but slower than the questions that kept popping up as I went — who did he fight the most ... where did he have the most fights ... who did he fight the longest in terms of years ... who did he avoid ... how many times was he on the side of law and order, and did he uphold his oath of office when he was?

My little spreadsheet on King's sound-era films shows that he was in 254 westerns, 39 serials, 31 features, and four shorts for a total of 328 films. I'm confident he had more in each category ... just walking across the lot at Columbia would have exposed him to more shorts than that, and, while I'm pretty sure all of his Republic stuff is there, I expect he is lurking around in a few Columbia and Universal serials that I haven't screened. There also may be a Western or two missing. I've also got a character name and role attached to Charlie on all but eight of the 328 roles.

So, unless he turns out to be named Blackie in those missing eight (none of which are Westerns or serials), the guy who most of us always called Blackie, before we even knew his name or could read credits, only answered to that name in nine — I counted them — films. Before starting, I figured on finding at least 20 or more. I didn't count Constable Black or Jim Black as being the same as Blackie. But not finding more than nine Blackies isn't what surprised me as much as the fact that he was called Red the same number of times. I can live with the name associated with him getting tied for multiple uses by another name, but it turns out that Blackie and Red are only tied for second and third place on the name parade. Some hero or another said to King, "I wouldn't do that if I were you, 'STEVE'" one more time than they offered the same advice to Blackie or Red. (I haven't used an exclamation point in print for over 30 years, but I was nearly tempted to there.)

Of course, a rose is a rose by any name — I don't have the same discipline with clichés as I do exclamation points — so, Charlie, by whatever name Tex or Ken offered the advice to, stayed true to character, disregarded it completely, and got stomped one more time. As it turns out, he also got chastised severely while answering to Joe or Jim seven times and Trigger on six occasions. He tried back-to-back Jakes in a couple of Lone Riders, and didn't fare any better leaving one to figure that George Houston, on the way out, tipped Bob Livingston, on the way in, to keep an eye on the guy called Jake.

There were lots of other multiple-used names including Tex three times and Ed five. In GHOST OF HIDDEN VALLEY, he was Ed 'Blackie' Decker, and I check marked both columns. Butch and Duke and Ace got hit more than once, but less than five. He got tagged with Vic a couple of times, but everybody that worked as villains in PRC Westerns eventually caught a Vic. That isn't, and never was, a standard B-Western villain handle, and I first thought it was just a PRC thing. But it also popped up on rare occasions at Republic, Columbia, and Monogram. Turns out to be a Fred Myton thing as his fingerprints, a couple of exceptions, are on all the Vic-is-the-villain scripts. Pure speculation on my part, but it appears that somebody named Vic got on Myton's bad side. I already checked on the possibility of a Victor Adamson (Denver Dixon) project gone sour.

Columbia serials gave King his best-name-against-type as Sir Edgar Bullard (in SON OF THE GUARDSMEN), Silk Landon (in THE IRON CLAW) and Ivor (in BRUCE GENTRY) and he responded to, after being called several times, Frenchy, in Monogram's HONOR OF THE MOUNTED. On cast-against-type, I found four sheriffs, two deputies, three policemen, two constables (RCMP type), and one detective.

PRC only existed for about seven years, but King evidently never went home during that period as he did 75 films there. His 57 at Monogram pale in comparison both numerically and on yearly average as those stretch across 20 years. With 46 at Columbia and 43 for Republic, King did nearly 65% of his films on just four lots. Harry Webb, A. W. Hackel, and Ed Finney signed most of the rest of his paychecks.

Speaking of Ed Finney, another childhood belief was that Tex Ritter beat up Charles King every 30 minutes and only stopped long enough to allow Buster Crabbe a shot or two. Neither threw more punches at the performer-formerly-known-as-Blackie than Battlin' Bob Steele who contested him on 29 occasions. The latter also holds the record for kicking King over the longest period of years, 16 beginning in 1930 through 1946. Buster took him on 24 times, and Tex is third at 23.

The purists among us might discount some of the Steele and Ritter work as the numbers include their "Trail Blazers" and "Texas Rangers" trio entries where they clearly had him out-numbered. My personal opinion is that it might be so in the case of Steele, but Ritter with Guy Wilkerson along was more hampered than helped.

For the most amounts of punches thrown in the shortest amount of time strictly mano-a-mano, Buster Crabbe wins the Charlie King sweepstakes. The 20 bouts staged by King and Johnny Mack Brown edge out the 18 total "Texas Rangers" for fourth place. But other than their Supreme and Republic stuff for A.

W. Hackel, King was usually just one of the gang in his other Brown films and wasn't Johnny's main concern. Brown usually just told Bob Baker or Fuzzy Knight to take care of Blackie, and he'd handle the main guys. Good thing he shared him, as Baker never had a solo shot at King in his starring films.

I can only find King in four of the "Frontier Marshals", so Charlie either took a couple of days off in 1942, or somebody at PRC decided that King against Bill "Cowboy Rambler" Boyd and Art Davis was an overmatch in favor of King. An overmatch must have been what King thought "Hopalong Cassidy" was, as I have no record of King in any entry of that series. He was in

Ken Maynard prevents Charlie from getting the girl.

Tom Tyler breaks up King's strangle hold.

the 1935, Republic/Winchester feature BURNING GOLD with Bill Boyd, but stayed clear of the Bar 20.

Another player usually often associated with King was Ken Maynard, but those two only tangled 16 times including three "Trail Blazers" when Maynard was part. But King and Maynard did most of their debating over a short period of time in Maynard's Tiffany and KBS films of the early 30s, and the image hung on.

Buck Jones also took advantage of King's punch-absorption skills 14 times (including four "Rough Riders") with Tom Tyler's 12 shots making up the only other double-digit staging. The "Range Busters" are way down among the less-than-ten also-rans, but Ray Corrigan, while not in all of the "Range Busters" films that had King, got a couple of extra chances with THE PAINTED STALLION and 1945's THE WHITE GORILLA. The latter film may be the only time a player had both the starring role and the title role, and they weren't the same role.

Charles King as "Blackie"

1. ALIAS THE BAD MAN (1931-Tiffany-Ken Maynard) - 'Black Mike' Richards
2. THE MYSTERY OF THE HOODED HORSEMEN (1937-Grand National-Tex Ritter) - Blackie Devlin
3. FLAMING FRONTIERS (1938-Universal serial-Johnny Mack Brown) - Henchman Blackie
4. TERRY AND THE PIRATES (1940-Columbia serial-Granville Owen) - Henchman Blackie
5. BORDER ROUNDUP (1942-PRC-George Houston) - Henchman Blackie
6. BLAZING GUNS (1943-Monogram-"Trail Blazers") - Henchman Blackie
7. DEATH VALLEY RANGERS (1943-Monogram-"Trail Blazers") - Henchman Blackie
8. SONORA STAGECOACH (1944-Monogram-"Trail Blazers") - Blackie Reed
9. GHOST OF HIDDEN VALLEY (1946-PRC-Buster Crabbe) - Ed 'Blackie' Decker

Johnny Mack has King in his grasp, but he'd better watch out for Ethan Laidlaw (LAW OF THE RANGE, Universal, 1941).

SOME OF CHARLIE'S CLASSIC MOMENTS

See if you remember these classic moments from Charlie's films.

HEADIN' FOR THE RIO GRANDE (Grand National, 1936): When Charlie meets up with Tex Ritter, he rubs his stubble whiskers and says, "Some time somewhere I've crossed this hombre's path before."

THE WHITE STALLION (aka HARMONY TRAIL, (Walt Mattox, 1944)): After being accused of having stolen cattle), with a straight face he mutters, "If those cattle were stolen, I find myself a very injured person."

Another one from THE WHITE STALLION: King sends his henchmen out to get rid of Marshal Rocky Camron, "You can't miss him. He's a scrappy kind of a fellow – always looking for trouble." Although addressed at Camron, it pretty much describes King himself.
Also a scene from the same film shows a close-up of hands arranging flowers. When the camera draws back, moviegoers are shocked to see that King is the arranger.

BILLY THE KID WANTED (PRC, 1941): Rival heavy Glenn Strange threatens King after he tries to muscle in on his operation, Charlie exclaims (mockingly), "Oh, don't, you know how timid I am of the law."

THREE IN THE SADDLE (PRC, 1945): King lunges at Guy Wilkerson with a knife, and Wilkerson pleads, "Aw, come on, have a heart." To which Charlie replies, "I'm going to – *yours*."

OUTLAWS OF THE PLAINS (PRC, 1946): King says to Fuzzy St. John: "I ain't killed a guy in over a week, and I wouldn't trust you with myself if I was you."

SING COWBOY, SING (Grand National, 1937): Just before his big fight with Tex Ritter, Charlie utters the classic line, "This town ain't big enough for you and me."

Prune-faced Earl Dwire, Tex Ritter, and Charlie are having a reflective moment (RIDERS OF THE ROCKIES, Grand National, 1937).

THEY WORKED WITH CHARLIE KING

Kirk Alyn (The screen's first "Superman"): Some days, the shooting of Westerns was a lot more full of fighting than others. There's a knack to making a fight seem convincing without ruining the faces of the cast for the next day's work. I counted up to 250 fights in which I took part without hurting anyone or getting hurt myself. There was one fellow who was an especially clever fist slinger named Charlie King. He looked the toughest of all the bad guys in the business, but, actually, one of the gentlest. On this particular day, everyone in the cast was feeling especially good. There had been just one fight after another, a most satisfying day's work.

But the next morning when we all turned up bright and early, Charlie seemed way down in the dumps. I asked him if anything was wrong, or did he feel bad? "I'm feeling lousy," he said. "Anything any of us did?" "No, no, not that," he moaned, and then he told me the whole story. "I went home last night and my cute little wife – I love that little gal – she had my dinner all ready. She fixed me a drink, and asked how everything went. I told her, 'Great, we had the best fights yet.' She handed me the drink, and said, 'Charlie, please be careful in those fights. I don't want you to get hurt.' "Aw honey", I said, "don't you worry about a thing. I've done hundreds of them, and nobody ever gets hurt. Look, I'll show you how we do it. You stand right there now. The camera is over there," and I pointed to a spot.

"Now when I throw a punch at somebody, I miss them about so much" – measuring off about a half inch with my front fingers. "Now stand still." I got down with a real swing, a right to the jaw. I knocked her colder than a cucumber – my cute little wife! In my whole life, I never miscued before, but I had to hit her. Do I feel lousy!"

(King appeared with Kirk Alyn in the first "Superman" serial (Columbia, 1948)).

Kirk Alyn

Bill "Cowboy Rambler" Boyd (Boyd made six films in the "Frontier Marshals" series, starring Lee Powell, Art Davis, and himself): Charlie, like a lot of stars, had a fondness for strong drink. It got so bad sometimes that he would go out in the shade behind one of those big rocks and drink. When they called for him back on the set, he would yell out, "Go to hell." He would come back to work though.

A 1942 publicity still of Bill "Cowboy Rambler" Boyd. He, along with Lee Powell and Art Davis formed a trio called the "Frontier Marshals."

Once while making RAIDERS OF THE WEST (PRC, 1942), Charlie was having one of those fights with Lee Powell down in a basement. Lee accidentally hit Charlie so hard that it sprained Lee's wrist. Charlie was knocked back, and hit his head on the edge of a chair. It took 12 stitches to close up the wound on Charlie's head. The scene was left in, and, if you look closely, you can see it. Another thing I remember about Charlie – and I swear it is the truth – he had this old horse that kept missing its mark (a designated spot where the director wants the horse to be). Charlie got off the horse, walked over, and whispered something in its ear. I don't know what he told the horse – maybe that it was headed for the glue factory – but whatever it was, it sure worked. The horse hit its mark perfectly the next time.

Eddie Dean (He related a similar story about Lee Powell's lack of screen fighting ability): I did a picture with Lee Powell in which I had to fight him. He was awfully rough to fight with because he didn't know how to pull a punch. He'd hit you! The other actors tipped me off. They said, "Don't let him hit you; he's big! Don't let him hit you because he doesn't know how to fight without hitting somebody. He doesn't know how to angle it." There was quite an

Eddie Dean

art to doing picture fights without getting hurt. I studied the technique so I wouldn't get hurt. I think I worked on the last picture Lee Powell made – at least one of the very last.

I suppose Charlie King was my favorite badman. I know a lot of people like Roy Barcroft, but Roy wasn't in any of my pictures. Charlie was surely a lot of fun to be around.

Lash LaRue: The only one who could fight better than me in pictures was Charlie King (laugh). He was a likable guy. He

Eddie Dean, Lash LaRue, and Bobby Copeland at Charlotte, 1985.

Charlie plays the sheriff in this Lash LaRue Film (LAW OF THE LASH, PRC, 1947).

drank a lot, but it never interfered with his work. I think the bottle really got to him in his later years. I wish I could have worked with him more.

Sunset Carson: Charlie King and I were on tour in a little town in Oklahoma. One morning, we went to this little restaurant for breakfast. Charlie was feeling a little rough from too much to drink the night before. When we got through eating and headed back to the car, two kids came walking down the road. They looked us over and on said, "Hey, that's Sunset Carson!'" The other one said, "And that's that mean old badman; let's get him!" They picked up some rocks, and started throwing them at poor old Charlie. He had to run to the car for cover.

Handsome Sunset Carson made some of Republic's most action-filled films.

Bob Steele: I took Black Jack O'Shea on most of my personal appearances. I know everyone was used to seeing me mix it up with Charlie King, but Charlie drank too much for me to take him on the road with me.

Charlie left no room for doubt; he always let you know how he felt. He was a great guy. In fact, many other heavies and some heroes learned a lot from Charlie King. He was so much fun in real life. In those days when we were all together so much, we became one happy family. If there was any larking around off-screen, you can be sure Charlie was in the middle of it. He was a big man — not too tall — but he weighed over 200 pounds. He was great to do fights with — so agile for a man his size.

It seems every time Charlie looks around, he sees Bob Steele (LAST OF THE WARRENS, Supreme, 1936).

Charlie (called Badger in this film) is getting set straight by Battling Bob. To the left, Phyllis Adair and Carleton Young (BILLY THE KID'S FIGHTING PALS, PRC, 1941).

(Perhaps Steele was a drinking buddy of Charlie's, since Steele himself was an alcoholic for a number of years. Friend and fellow actor Dana Andrews (an alcoholic too) persuaded Steele to attend Alcoholics Anonymous with him. Steele got straightened out and was off the booze for the last 20 years of his life.)

Tris Coffin

Tris Coffin: Charlie King and Bud Osborne were close friends, and they were heavy drinkers. Over the years, I worked with both of them many times but I never knew of either one to louse up a scene, or a day's shooting due to their drinking.

Glenn Strange in his "Gunsmoke" attire.

Glenn Strange: He enjoyed himself in these lighter roles. He was a funny man off-screen, and could easily have scored in comedy films. He had a natural flair for comedy, and would have been great in something like the "Keystone Kops".

Buster Crabbe: Charlie was a big man, but he was as agile as a cat. He moved like a gazelle. He fought a lot of the movie cowboys and always lost, but I doubt any of them could have whipped

Buster Crabbe is distracted while walloping Charlie.

him in a real fight. I know I wouldn't have wanted to take him on. He was not only agile; he was very fast for a big man, and

Oliver Drake

as strong as an ox. If he had been more serious about his career, and laid off the booze, he might have been a big star. He certainly had the talent.

Oliver Drake (director): (Regarding his work with comic Guy Wilkerson and King): I remember we did one picture (ENEMY OF THE LAW (PRC, 1945)) where they put him (Guy Wilkerson) in jail with an outlaw to try to find out where the outlaw had hidden a treasure. The outlaw,

Charlie King, draws a map to the treasure on the bottom of Guy's foot while he's asleep. A little while later, they escape together. Wilkerson, not knowing anything about the map, takes off his socks, and throws them away, and washes his feet. Well, the map ends up on the bottom of the socks, and, fortunately, the socks are retrieved and the treasure eventually found. Charlie was really great in the picture. (This was one of King's best villain/comic roles.)

Pierce Lyden: One day at Columbia, I bumped into Charlie King, one of the great all-time heavies in pictures. All the B-Western movie fans knew him as "Blackie". He had a good sense of humor, loved a practical joke, and liked to clown around. He was a partaker of the "fruit of the vine", and, on this particular incident, it was one of those times.

He hadn't any more than said hello when we saw a ragpicker (wardrobe men were often referred to as "Rags" or "Ragpicker") we knew coming down the street. Blackie says, "Let's put this guy on. He wouldn't let anyone in his last picture wear a neckerchief." Sure enough Rags didn't even have time to say hello.

He was obviously hyped up. "I've just made history!" he says, like he had found a simple way to stop a stampede. "It's never been done in Westerns!" There's no doubt he was riding high and looking ahead for a big raise he was going to ask the studio for after he got his Oscar at the Academy Awards. "No, sir, it's never been done. I wouldn't let a cowboy on the picture wear a neckerchief around his neck."

About that time, Charlie, who is getting impatient, says,

Pierce Lyden demonstrates his evil stare.

Bobby and Joan Copeland with Pierce Lyden (Charlotte, 1984).

"Well, I'll see you around. Guess you won't be here much longer." Rags says, "What?" And Charlie comes back with, "I hear the front end (studio head) has been told that the real cowboys and the young ones will laugh themselves silly." And when Rags says, "What are you guys talking about?"

We proceeded to take turns telling him of the horrible consequences of a cowboy without a bandana to cover his face on the cattle drive with a snowstorm cutting his face and ears to the bone, or a sandstorm grinding and tearing the flesh away. And down at the river, what would we do for a washrag? Or maybe it would cost him an arm or a leg if he couldn't whip off his neckerchief to make a tourniquet for snakebite. He might also need it for a sling for a broken arm or to stop the flow of blood from a wound. A cowboy without a neckerchief was just too gruesome to contemplate." We were really rolling, and there was much more. Rags was shifting around from one foot to another. He was all but talking to himself now. We couldn't tell if he wanted to laugh or cry. About this time, as I remember,

Charlie wound up with something like, "It's not your fault Rags, you just didn't know any better. You're not one of us cowboys." Charlie and I laughed about that for a long time.

Frances Kavanaugh (writer): We used Charlie King whenever we could. He was a good actor.

Ken Maynard is not explaining the facts of life to Blackie.

THEY'RE WRITING ABOUT CHARLIE KING

The Old Corral (Letter from Tom Bahn who is married to Charles "Slim" Whitaker's great-granddaughter Debbie): Leota (Whitaker's daughter) remembers that Wally Wales (better known as Hal Taliaferro), Charlie King, and Al Bridge were like her uncles. She commented that it was as if they lived there. Charlie lived on Bellaire Street, and Slim lived approximately two miles north on Hatteras Street, in North Hollywood. North Hollywood was quite a bit different in the 1930s. The San Fernando Valley was predominately horse ranches, cattle ranches, orange groves, and farms. Charlie and Al were regular drinking buddies of Slim's, and the drinking parties and poker games were always at Slim's place.

In 1986, Debbie and I drove by Slim and Charlie's old places. It was apparent the old neighborhood had been bulldozed in the 1950s, and tract homes were built. Charlie's property had an expensive single story ranch house built on it.

Hollywood Corral by Don Miller (Regarding King's role in the Ken Maynard film DEATH RIDES THE RANGE (Colony, 1940): The film is notable otherwise for the absolute running amok by Charlie King as one of the baddies; King waylays every actor in sight at about the three-quarter mark, becoming a one-man blitzkrieg and taking the action honors away from Ken com-

Steele tries his trick roping on King (BILLY THE KID'S FIGHTING PALS, PRC, 1941).

pletely, if indeed there were any honors to take.

(Regarding King's work with Bob Steele): Veteran Charlie King was more often than not on the receiving end of the Steele wrath throughout their careers, and King must have spent leisure time figuring out how to receive yet another Steele flurry of blows in a different manner. What made Steele's tasks all the more difficult was his lack of size. It was necessary for him to make the audience believe that he could knock about some huge bear of a baddie without getting squashed in the process. This he invariably did, so it was perhaps his highest achievement in Westerns. It also gave every little kid hope in a world that seemed at times peopled with bullies.

The Filming of the West by Jon Tuska (Regarding the 1933 Universal picture, STRAWBERRY ROAN): Frank Yaconelli and Charles King were Ken Maynard's saddle pals and, oddly enough, musical support. Charlie had a rather brutal heavy role in Ken's films for Tiffany, but his role in *Roan* is one of the very few that fully appreciated his latent talent for comic and humorous by-play. Typecasting, unfortunately, defeated what hope Charlie may have had in pursuing this direction.

He constantly overspent the $125 a week he was paid and was always negotiating small loans from Ken and others. Charlie's untrusting wife would march up to the pay window on Fridays, and collect Charlie's wages. But Charlie was a free spirit who bore his wife's watchful eye with a shrug of his shoulders.

Saturday Afternoon at the Movies by Alan G. Barbour: I must pay tribute to one special actor who was nearly everyone's choice as the favorite Western villain of all time — Charles King. As the years went on, King gained more weight, too much in fact, and eventually found himself playing the role of a buffoon more than menace, much to the chagrin of all of us.

The Filming of the West by Jon Tuska: No matter who the principal villain was, Charlie King was always his (Tex Ritter's) right-hand man, and invariably the screenplay called for a stirring, even dramatic bout of fisticuffs between Tex and Charlie. Tex rarely had a stand-in for these fight sequences. Charlie taught him what there was to learn about fighting before the camera, and the two found it splendid fun.

Cliffhanger by Alan G. Barbour (Regarding King's role in the 1940 Columbia serial THE SHADOW): Too often comedy got in the way of the action when, for example, bad guy Charles King announces to his gang, "I had him (The Shadow) right where I wanted him, and then everything went black, whereupon he staggers around like a "Keystone Kop" and then falls backwards over a hedge. This kind of stuff was for two-reel comedies, not serials.

(It appears the author contradicts himself when writing about

the 1949 Columbia serial ADVENTURES OF SIR GALAHAD):
Part of the fun of watching this serial was in seeing Charles
King play a comic foil – a type of role he began his career with
in silent films. King engaged in various slapstick sequences,
even donning a dress when the situation called for such an
extreme.

Battlin' Bob Steele by Mario DeMarco: Charles King, my favorite, as countless other fans will claim, was a real "action"
villain. Way back in the 1940s I talked to a group of Western
extras. Hank Bell (the character actor with the big handlebar
mustache) was one of them, and we got on the subject of
badmen. Hank told me that the work at the studios was really
good, and "It beat punching cattle at a mere $40.00 a month."
When we got to the subject of Charlie King, Hank told me he
was one of the nicest guys around, and that his biggest prob-
lem was "whooping" it up with his many buddies, which usually
ended up with them having to take him home. He said Charlie's
wife usually collected his pay at the studio before Charlie could
get it—for obvious reasons.

The Bad Guys by William K. Everson: Round-faced, black
mustached Charles King rapidly became the apotheosis of all
Western villains. Equally at home playing the "big boss" in a
tailored suit or lowly unshaven minion in torn and dirty jeans,
he was successfully pulverized in climatic fist fights by every
Western star in the business from Ken Maynard and Buck Jones
through Tex Ritter, Gene Autry, Johnny Mack Brown, and even
Lash LaRue. Few non-Western aficionados knew his name,
but almost any moviegoer would identify him as "Blackie" —
the semi-symbolic name he invariably used.

Chuck Anderson's website: I've always separated King's
career into three rather arbitrary periods:
- His "youthful" period, roughly the decade of the 1930s,
  when he was still somewhat slim.
- His "boss baddie" years around the early 1940s, when he

had gained some weight, but had graduated to portraying the primary villain ... and this often required him to wear a suit.

- His later years, beginning around the end of World War II, when he had gotten noticeably older and heavier, and shifted to comedic roles.

My fondest remembrances of Charlie King are those great fight scenes, generally in 1930s era sagebrushers where he would pummel — and be pummeled — by the likes of Bob Steele, Buster Crabbe, and Tex Ritter. Some folks even compared Charlie to a punching bag. I can still recall Charlie King's long, straight hair flopping in his face during those wonderful screen brawls.

King's sound-era credits number about 300 film appearances, mostly westerns and serials. This includes about 45 westerns and serials at Republic Pictures from 1935 - 1949.

Charlie makes a point to Bob Steele while Kermit Maynard, John Cason, and Syd Saylor look on. Charlie is called "Al" in the movie (AMBUSH TRAIL, PRC, 1946).

THE FANS SPEAK UP FOR CHARLIE

I have asked some of the most knowledgeable fans of B-Westerns and serials to offer their comments on King's place and rating in the movies. I realize there is some duplication in the comments, which is to be expected when discussing the same individual, but I did not think it appropriate to edit the material. The following are the results of my inquiries:

Richard B. Smith III (author/researcher): Charles King must be classified among the "Top Five" of those most recognized B-Western movie villains from that 1930s-1940s Golden Age cinema era who gave many headaches to Saturday-matinee cowboy heroes with his never ending skullduggery involving holdups, rustling, ore pilfering, land grabbing, etc.

More affectionately remembered using character names like "Red," "Blackie," "Trigger," and "Steve", King could be equally menacing on horseback as both main boss of a scheming gang or just plain dog heavy. Charlie found semi-regular studio employment in 1938 with Monogram Pictures, although his appearances throughout the earlier part of the first eight years of this decade included acting stints at Republic, Supreme, and Ambassador. And who could ever forget his endless scuffles at less-moneyed PRC—mainly Charlie's movie home from 1940 -1947—against Tex Ritter, George Houston, Bob Livingston, and Buster Crabbe among others.

King's stomach became bigger the more he gained weight, and was it ever an invitable target by Bob Steele with his quick jabs! Charlie endured loads of physical scenes, but I feel his most challenging part came with Gene Autry's GOLD MINE IN THE SKY (Republic, 1938). Madcap convertible driver Carol Hughes splashes Charlie, a building painter, with very liquid mud over his entire body several different times. He certainly passed the patience test here.

This perennial tough guy could always be recognized regardless of role size as the miscreant with thick, dark eyebrows and ever-present mustache. Monogram pulled "a sneak play" with one of "The Trail Blazers" entries, WESTWARD BOUND (1944), which allowed an uncredited King to double recognized baddie Harry Woods in a bruising fight scene with Bob Steele.

It's interesting to note that Charlie was also inserted into the last starring B-Westerns of three cowboys he always battled at PRC – Tex Ritter (FLAMING BULLETS, 1945), Bob Steele (THUNDER TOWN, 1946), and Buster Crabbe (OUTLAWS OF THE PLAINS, 1946). Charles got into his only two tint B-Westerns that used Cinecolor at PRC, each starring singing cowboy Eddie Dean. They were THE CARAVAN TRAIL and COLORADO SERENADE, both 1946 releases. As the 1940s waned, and average minimal-costing oaters were becoming less of a Saturday matinee B-commodity, King did more supports in Columbia and Republic serials to justify his salary needs. One memorable moment for Charlie in SON OF ZORRO (Republic, 1947) occurs at conclusion of Chapter 11, "The Devil's Trap," where he joins an even more evil-minded Roy Barcroft to help shove a blazing haywagon down one backlot alleyway to cremate masked Zorro character George Turner.

Charles King inserted himself into over 250 B-Westerns over a 20-year period. However, the biggest mystery remains as to why he never made it onto television's little screen by 1949 or 1950 with any of his old saddle buddies and do roles for this new broadcast medium's half-hour Western shows. But, what-

A mustached Bob Steele is corralled by Bud Geary, King and another badman (THUNDER TOWN, PRC, 1946).

ever the reason, Charles King still left a major screen impact, which continues to resonate today in the early 21st century. A devoted, loyal following of his Western fans sees to that.

Boyd Magers (editor *Western Clippings):* Charles King is, without a doubt, the preeminent bad-man of '30s and '40s B-westerns. In the early years, Charlie alternated between wearing a thick black mustache or being clean-shaven. It was quite obvious he was always fighting the 'battle of the bulge' but still maintained a good figure until the late '30s when he must have decided to 'let it all hang out'. His paunchy potbelly and ever growing mustache (which flowered to full old-west droopiness in many PRC titles), and often baggy-pants western garb endeared him to several generations of front row kids.

In his nearly 300 westerns he had the opportunity to play every type of villain from suave banker or saloon owner to the nastiest, black-hearted, dog-kicker of them all. Charles Lafayette King, Jr., was born February 21, 1895, in Hillsboro, TX, the son of a Kentucky born physician. His father wanted Charles to follow in his footsteps but Charlie chose acting instead.

At age 20 (or possibly younger) Charlie was in Hollywood with his earliest supposed work as an extra in BIRTH OF A NATION (1915). His first recorded film work was as a bartender in the 1921 comedy A MOTION TO ADJOURN with Roy Stewart. He supported William Russell the same year in SINGING RIVER. THE PRICE OF YOUTH and THE BLACK BAG followed in 1922. One of his earliest, if not his first, western roles was opposite Lester Cuneo in HEARTS OF THE WEST ('25). From there he was seen menacing Fred Humes and Bill Cody in silent oaters.

Before Charlie really became established in westerns he had a run at being a comedian in Universal's popular Mike and Ike two-reel comedy shorts of the late '20s.

Researcher Ken Weiss found this notice in the September 1928 *Universal Weekly*, a studio in-house publication.

Charles King Arrives in New York for First Visit.
Charles King, better known on screen as 'Mike' of the Stern Brothers' 'Mike and Ike, They Look Alike' comedies, is visiting New York for the first time. Accompanied by his wife, whose stage name is Dorothy Murray, they are visiting relatives in her hometown, Brooklyn. King plans to remain here for ten days before returning to Universal City to start a new series of the Mike and Ike comedies. His wife has been engaged for a tour of the Publix Theaters in a song and dance act under the title of 'The Little Girl with the High Silk Hat'. When not clowning in Universal comedies, King plays leading roles in dramatic productions, having recently completed 'Sisters of Eve' with Betty Blythe.

(Incidentally, Charlie's early screen credits are often confused with those of an English actor by the same name who died in 1944.) Charlie's comedic flair was often demonstrated in Westerns — especially the Dave O'Brien/Tex Ritter PRC series (in particular ENEMY OF THE LAW and CARAVAN TRAIL with Eddie Dean and Al (Lash) LaRue.

With the advent of sound, Charlie found himself solidly ensconced and well-received in hordes of B-Westerns opposite Ken Maynard, Buck Jones, Bob Steele, Tim McCoy, Rex Bell, Hoot Gibson, Gene Autry, Kermit Maynard, Tom Tyler and others. His barroom brawls with, first, Bob Steele then Tex Ritter became legendary screen battles we all eagerly anticipated.

Although all the studios employed him, PRC and Monogram kept Charlie the busiest in the '40s in feature after feature, daunting the likes of Buster Crabbe, Lee Powell, James Newill, Dave O'Brien, George Houston, Johnny Mack Brown, the "Rough Riders," Tom Keene, Lash LaRue, "Trail Blazers", "Range Busters", and others. Older (now in his early 50s) and heavier, always fighting a well-known battle with booze, Charlie found work harder to come by as the B-Westerns which had been his steady form of income faded from the screen.

A role in OKLAHOMA BLUES with Jimmy Wakely seems to be his last, although he can be spotted in smaller roles in bigger budget films such as WYOMING and Abbott and Costello's WISTFUL WIDOW OF WAGON GAP (both '47).

Charlie had found work in serials since WHAT HAPPENED TO JANE in 1926 and continued to do so with CONGO BILL ('48), ADVENTURES OF SIR GALLAHAD ('49) (again displaying his true comic talent) and BRUCE GENTRY ('49).

Despondent and out of work, Charlie attempted suicide on February 15, 1951, only days before his 56th birthday, according to an *Los Angeles Evening Herald and Express* 2/16/51 article (Thanks to G. D. Hamann.): Charlie "gazed upon the peaceful scene of his family gathered in the living room at 539 North Arden Blvd. watching television. Tears coursed down his cheeks as he entered the room and announced, 'I love you all, goodbye!' Then he stalked dramatically out and, a few moments later, the family heard a (gunshot) report and rushed into the bathroom to discover Charlie had shot himself in the chest with his son's .22 caliber rifle. He was too rugged for that, however. Police said the bullet coursed around his ribs and out his back and that his injury was not critical. No reason was given (to police) for his act.

Following his recovery and during his final years, Charlie appeared as an extra on early episodes of "Gunsmoke" (watch for him right behind James Arness as a courtroom observer in "Custer", drinking a beer in the barroom in "Man Who Would Be Marshal" and "Jealousy", sitting in a chair in "Liar From Blackhawk".)

It's often been said King died while playing a corpse on the James Arness series, or minutes thereafter. However, this is doubtless the stuff of which western "urban legends" are born, as I've personally never seen a "Gunsmoke" where King played a corpse. The other fact that makes this unlikely is the time of his death on May 7, 1957 at 7:45 pm. Not that they couldn't have been filming this late, it's just more unlikely. Also, Charlie died at 62 of a hepatic coma brought on by cirrhosis and chronic alcoholism at John Wesley County Hospital. At the time he was divorced and living at 4914 Bellaire Ave. in N. Hollywood. (His son, Charles S. King, was killed in the '80s at an early age when he surprised a man burglarizing his apartment.) If only Charlie had lived to realize he was the heavy we loved to hate, I think he would have been pleased.

Paul Dellinger (author): Charlie King never looked exactly like a villain to me. He was a little too rotund, even with his black hat and black mustache, for me to believe he was a match for the hero. However, as soon as he began to act, I forgot all about that and realized immediately what a menace he was. He made more movies than ace villain Roy Barcroft did. And because Barcroft was tied by a contract to a single studio (Republic) for so long, King got to tangle with even more Western movie heroes than did Barcroft. Often, King and Barcroft would be part of the same gang. Example: BORDERTOWN GUN FIGHTERS (Republic, 1943) with Wild Bill Elliott, Gabby Hayes, and Harry Woods as good guys (Woods was usually a villain – in fact, he was the villain of whom Barcroft said he patterned his own bad guys – but this time he was a U. S. marshal). Charlie King played a crooked sheriff, and Barcroft was his crooked deputy. The big shootout has the sheriff's office ready to serve phony warrants on Bill and his friends so they can shoot them while "resisting arrest." As Bill, Gabby, and Woods come toward the crooked deputies down the street, King suddenly thrusts the warrants in Barcroft's hands. "You serve them!" he orders, and Barcroft hesitates just long enough to get a laugh from the audience. "And while he's doing that, you boys take 'em," he tells the rest of the gang. Then he goes and hides.

King's villainous characters were usually more than able to do their own dirty deeds. As unromantic as he looked, he would still try to force the heroine into a marriage (usually more for

Bill Elliott and Gabby Hayes with three of the baddest of the B-Western badmen, Roy Barcroft, Harry Woods, and King (BORDERTOWN GUNFIGHTERS, Republic, 1943).

Fuzzy takes on Bob Cason, while Buster Crabbe is about to land a haymaker on Charlie. King is called Cal in this picture (PRAIRIE BADMEN, PRC, 1946).

financial than romantic reasons) until Bob Steele arrived in the nick of time. He also tangled with Buck Jones, Ken Maynard, Bill Cody, Hoot Gibson, Tom Tyler, Tim McCoy, Jack Hoxie, Rex Bell, John Wayne, Tom Keene, Bob Custer, Kermit Maynard, Tom Mix, Gene Autry, Johnny Mack Brown, George O'Brien, Tex Ritter, Jack Randall, Fred Scott, Lee Powell, James Newill, Roy Rogers, Don Barry, George Houston, Buster Crabbe, Tim Holt, Robert Livingston, Charles Starrett, Richard Arlen, Sunset Carson, Eddie Dean, Lash LaRue, Kirby Grant, Clayton Moore, and Jimmy Wakely, among others less well known.

In MARKED FOR MURDER (PRC, 1944), he plays a more flamboyant-than-usual killer Wild Charlie Gray (given the name, one wonders if the role wasn't written for him). When he gets out of prison, Tex Ritter and Dave O'Brien are on his trail to see where he buried his loot. They plant comic sidekick Panhandle Perkins (Guy Wilkerson) in his cell to gain his confidence. Unknown to Panhandle, Charlie destroys his map so it

Bob Steele has just put King's lights out (LIGHTNIN' CRANDALL, Republic 1937).

won't be found on him when he is released, and reproduces it in ink on Panhandle's foot while Panhandle is sleeping. Comedy abounds after that as Charlie becomes protective of Panhandle to the bafflement of the rest of the gang, and horrified when Panhandle decides that he wants a bath. You almost felt sorry for Charlie when, believing Panhandle is his buddy, let's Panhandle lead him right into a jail cell at the end. The disappointment in his face is both hilarious and sad.

But just to keep the audience aware of his deadliness, he ruthlessly murders a surgeon earlier in the story after the doctor has supposedly removed an identifying scar from him.

He is similarly ruthless in HIS BROTHER'S GHOST (PRC, 1945), a Buster Crabbe movie in which Al St. John plays a double role – his patented Fuzzy Q. Jones character and Andy Jones, Fuzzy's twin brother. When Charlie King's gang kills

Andy, Fuzzy assumes his identity, and frightens various members who think they are seeing a ghost. When one of them insists on leaving the gang, he assures King he won't tell what he knows about his crimes. "No," King agrees; he doesn't think the man will, and calmly shoots him in the back. Then he asks if anybody else has any crazy ideas about leaving. No one does.

King appeared in a number of serials, especially toward the end of his career, the last being Columbia's THE GREAT ADVENTURES OF CAPTAIN KIDD (1953). Four years earlier, he had actually played a comic sidekick as Sir Boors in Columbia's ADVENTURES OF SIR GALAHAD, with George Reeves, TV's future "Superman". Still earlier, he appeared with the screen's first "Superman", Kirk Alyn.

Dale Berry (actor): Bill "Cowboy Rambler" Boyd, Art Davis, and Lee Powell made six features called "The Frontier Marshals" for Producers Releasing Corporation in 1942. I think

Art Davis is trying to untie Bill Boyd, but Charlie gets the drop on him (TUMBLEWEED TRAIL, PRC, 1942).

Charlie King was in all of them. Charlie was one of Bill Boyd's favorite people. He told me that on one of the pictures he was doing a fight with Charlie. The scene called for Bill to hit Charlie with a vicious haymaker, and Charlie was supposed to go flying over a couch or something. Bill was then to run over and reach behind the couch, pull Charlie up, and smack him again. Bill would nearly go into hysterics when telling the story of how when he reached to pick Charlie up, he was lying on the floor, looking up at Bill making faces at him – sticking out his tongue, flapping his ears, etc. This cracked Bill up so much that part of the scene had to be reshot. Being a cheap studio, and having to reshoot, I'm sure the director was not amused.

Around 1946, I was on my way to California, and Bill Boyd asked me to call some of his old friends. The first one he mentioned was Charlie King – others were John Cason and Glenn Strange. I regret that something came up, and I never made the calls.

Guy Wilkerson takes on Kermit Maynard while Tex Ritter subdues Jack Ingram, and Dave O'Brien has a great target in King's belly. Kay Hughes is on far right. Charlie plays "Charlie" in this film. (ENEMY OF THE LAW, PRC, 1945).

Fuzzy does double duty as he gets a footlock on Kermit Maynard and a headlock on John Cason. Buster only has to fight old Charlie (PRAIRIE BADMEN, PRC, 1946.)

George Coan (publisher, *The Old Time Cowboy Picture Show*): In a recent poll, by readers of *The Old Time Cowboy Picture Show*'s newsletter, Charlie King came in at second place, behind Roy Barcroft, of course, as favorite villain. Although his villainy is well documented, my favorite characterization by Charlie was as Pete Magoo in MARKED FOR MURDER (PRC 1944), A Tex Ritter extravaganza. Charlie should have been a sidekick. He was well adept at comedy, and used his talents in several films that needed his help badly. Long live the King, Charlie that is.

Jim Hamby (long-time Western movie and film festival fan): Charles King as a heavy – great, as the leader of the gang – good. He is probably one of the best-known Western and serial supporting actors of the '30s and '40s. I also remember him as being great with comedy. You could see the expression in his face even during his fight scenes with Bob Steele and

62

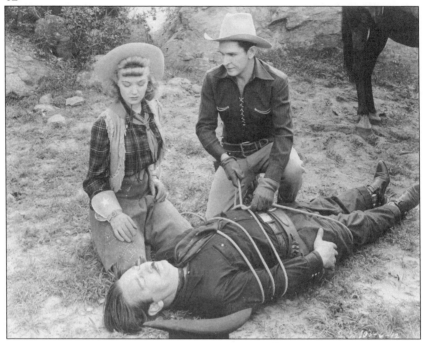

**Phyllis Adair and Bob Steele look on while Charlie is "counting stars"
(BILLY THE KID'S FIGHTING PALS, PRC, 1941).**

Tex Ritter.

He had some great comedy moments with Guy "Panhandle
Perkins" Wilkerson in the "Texas Rangers" series at PRC starring Tex Ritter and Dave O'Brien, and Wilkerson. He also had
many comic scenes with Fuzzy St. John in the Buster Crabbe
series. Would we (the fans) have accepted him in other comedy roles? I think so. Would we have enjoyed him as a perma-
nent sidekick to one of our Western heroes? I certainly would
have.

Bill Sasser (promoter Williamsburg Film Festival): My memory
of Charlie King is as a consummate badman. He could play
the lead heavy, the member of the gang, the buffoon, all with
skill and perfection. No better badman ever appeared on the
screen than "Blackie".

Grady Franklin (former publisher of *The Western Film*): We tend to be impressed easily in our youthful years. Sometimes, the emulation we have of others is in a negative way rather than that of a positive role model. When I was a movie-going boy in the '30s and '40s, I definitely did not look upon Charles King as a positive influence in my life. Shoot, it was a long time before I even knew he had two names like the rest of us. He answered to "Blackie" a lot.

How could a guy with that handle be a role model? When it wasn't Blackie, it was Butch, Ace, Pork, Bull, Scar, Creed, Silk, and the like. Those were not names folks in my part of East Tennessee went by during the years Charlie King was getting heavier and getting beat up most Saturdays at the Grand Theater. When I was at my front-row kid best, Charlie was being chased a lot by the likes of Tex Ritter, Bob Steele, and Buster Crabbe in B-Westerns turned out by Colony, Grand National, Monogram, and PRC. As I got older, advanced deeper into Boy Scouting, and developed many of life's values, there was

Charles King was called Dawson in this movie with Buster Crabbe and Al (Fuzzy) St. John (GHOST OF HIDDEN VALLEY, PRC, 1946) .

King looks on as Tex Ritter explains the situatiion to Horace Murphy and Snub Pollard. Charlie plays Butch in this movie (RIDERS OF THE ROCKIES, Grand National, 1937).

old Charlie getting clobbered in Columbia serials at the Ritz Theater.

If you thought you were seeing him everywhere you looked on the screen, it's because he was just about everywhere. One day, he'd be in a cowboy outfit. The next, he'd be in street clothes. Perhaps because he became so rotund, Charlie had a strange walk. Oh, nothing like that of Lash LaRue, but much different than a regular cowboy (maybe with the exception of John Wayne).

Charlie stood out in a crowd in other ways. His voice was easily recognized behind a mask or in darkness of night. By the way, if kids knew it was Charlie King behind that mask, why didn't those adults on the screen know it was that crook Blackie?

Some other villains who had distinct voices were Bud Osborne, Glenn Strange, Roy Barcroft, Forrest Taylor, Warner Richmond, and George Chesebro. There was no mistaking Charlie for any of those guys, or for the likes of Pierce Lyden, Ernie Adams, or Stan Jolley – mask or no mask.

Well, I got past Charlie, or at least didn't have him on my mind during those years when I thought more about girls, when I was in the Army, and when I became a husband and father. However, I re-discovered the whole gang — Charlie, Tex, Hoppy, Rex, Gene, Smiley, all of them — in the late '70s when I started going to Western film festivals. By then, the fans were treating Charlie, Pierce and Frosty (Terry Frost) like heroes. They would cheer when the "bad guy" images appeared on the screen or in the screening room in person. I never met Charlie in person. But I have met several guys at festivals who reminded me a lot of him. They were heavy, sometimes obnoxious, and oftentimes comedic — Charlie King traits in the living flesh.

But make no mistake: There was only one Charles King. Just

King is getting ready to make a loud noise (THE MAN FROM THUNDER RIVER, Republic, 1943).

Charlie finds himself in the grasp of Johnny Mack Brown (WEST OF CARSON CITY, Universal, 1940.)

as there was only one Al St. John, one Tex Ritter, or one Smiley Burnette. He worked hard in hundreds of movies and serials. He was dedicated and serious about his craft. Such devotion to one's profession should be emulated, and, for that aspect of his persona, I look up to him. This native Texan had a lot going for him, and should be remembered with respect and admiration.

John Leonard (author *Wild Bill Elliott*): Charlie King or "Blackie", as I knew him when I saw him on the screen as a kid, was always one of my favorite "bad guys", ranking, probably, fifth behind Roy Barcroft, Bud Geary, LeRoy Mason, and Dick Curtis. As a kid, for a long time I never knew his real name, only "Blackie", from an early role that I saw him in.

He may have been more versatile than some of the other "heavies". He played a variety of roles. Sometimes, he would be the lead heavy, especially at PRC and Monogram. Other times, he would have the part of the hero's sidekick. An example of this was with Bill Elliott in IN EARLY ARIZONA and THE LAW COMES TO TEXAS. Then he might be the comic relief, such as the "Texas Rangers" series at PRC with Dave O'Brien and/ or Jim Newill and Tex Ritter. Mostly his roles at Republic and Columbia were as the "henchie" or "work heavy".

One of my favorite roles of his was the part of Sheriff Barnes in BORDERTOWN GUN FIGHTERS. At the end, when the shooting is about to start, he gives his deputy Roy Barcroft the warrants to serve on Bill Elliott, Gabby Hayes, and Harry Woods, then, cowardly, goes back into his office, and shuts the door, leaving Barcroft and the rest to shoot it out with Wild Bill, Gabby, and Harry Woods.

Charlie had a long career in the B-Western era, and, I always felt, gave an entertaining performance

Bill Russell (author): I liked Charlie King. I loved the way he could get bounced around by Bob Steele or Tex Ritter, and by a host of other stars, and then come back for more. No matter how much punishment he took (and he could dish it out, too), if he had been a prizefighter, he would have a record something like 0-250, or however many films he took a beating in. Against Steele, he was 0-22 at my count.

The one thing I liked about Charlie was the fact that he was not your devious, evil-planning heavy like a Harry Woods, or smart gang-leader "brains" like a Roy Barcroft, or simply a no-account thug like Blackie Whiteford (another of my favorites heavies). He was often duped into confrontations that resulted in the obvious duke-it-out barroom brawl with the hero that the boss surely didn't want to get involved himself. Let Charlie do all the dirty work. And he did. Tough? He was more than tough! I don't think I ever saw him go down with one punch, no matter whom he was facing.

Charlie was more than just a member of the gang. You could

rank him as second-in-command, usually essaying the role of the field boss of the gang, the outlaw who carried the orders back to the gang members holed up in the shack back in the hills playing cards or just hanging around. King brought them orders, and they were on their way. Sometimes, Charlie would be the boss, decked out in suit and all, but more often than not, he was the main field "heavy".

I often wondered how Charlie, or "Blackie", as he was some-times known, handled it all physically. There were no stunt doubles for him, especially in the Steele brawls. They were beautifully choreographed scenarios that while staged must have taken a lot out of Charlie over the years.

Riley Hill, King, and Ethan Laidlaw seem to have Johnny Mack Brown under control. (LAW OF THE RANGE, Universal, 1944).

There was another side of Charlie King that many fans may not recall. Have you ever seen him in the 1933 Ken Maynard STRAWBERRY ROAN? You wouldn't believe it was the same character of several years later. Even then sometimes he would be on the side of the law or the hero. I recall in a couple of Columbia Bill Elliott's (IN EARLY ARIZONA, '38 and THE LAW COMES TO TEXAS, '39), he played good guys.

Charlie was also a scene-stealer. I remember one film, a 1940 Ken Maynard Colony, DEATH RIDES THE RANGE, when Maynard and Charlie did a lot of furniture busting and where King virtually runs amok, becoming a one-man force of destruction, totally taking the action honors away from Maynard.

But as the years wore on, and he got a little heavier, his roles took on more of the buffoon than a tough "henchie". Oh, he could still take a punch and go down, but it often seemed more of a comic action.

Nevertheless, there was only one Charlie King, the bad guy you often respected and maybe even secretly rooted for sometimes, but his forte was that of a brawler, and in that he excelled. And who can forget that low, raspy voice, much in the same, easily remembered and distinctive tones of Al Bridge.

According to Roy Liebman in his *From Silents to Sound*, King was an extra in silents from about 1915 before doing the "Mike and Ike" series (as he calls it). Reportedly, he made his first Western film debut in 1921 in the Fox film, SINGING RIVERS, starring William Russell. Another silent credit I have for him is a 1925 Ward Lascalle production called HEARTS OF THE WEST (not the Jeff Bridges version, obviously), starring Lester Cuneo. In 1926, he also made the first of many series, WHAT HAPPENED TO JANE (not "Baby Jane"). Anyway, Liebman writes that he appears (or was credited) in only a few features during the '20's, his last silent film being SLIM FINGERS in 1929. It should be noted, too, that Liebman points out that King's filmography is sometimes confused with, or even combined with, that of the stage singer Charles King (1894-1944).

A rare shot of King without his mustache.

Tinsley Yarbrough (author and Western film locations expert): If the meek ultimately inherit the earth, as Scriptures tell us, good ol' alcoholic Charlie will surely become a king! With few exceptions, he played the brains heavy only at PRC, the runt of the B-Western litter. Even there, he seldom rated the sort of period outfit oily Stan Jolley usually sported. Instead, Charlie was relegated to the '40s-style double-breasted suit he regularly wore in Columbia's chapterplays. Most of the time, it was Charlie's lot to play the dog heavy, regularly beaten senseless by our hero, rarely surviving until the end of the movie, and the butt of frequent jokes. Remember the scene in THE MYSTERY OF THE HOODED HORSEMEN? Members of the gang pounce upon a hooded interloper they suspect is Tex Ritter, beating him to a pulp. Then they unmask their victim – only to find the ever-hapless Charlie, not Tex, behind the mask! Every time I think of the look on Charlie's face in that scene, I chuckle. In fact, Charlie's comedic turns were often the highlight of the films he graced with his presence. Had he gone into comedy, he might have ascended heights. Of course, we front-row kids are glad he didn't. There were lots of comedy kings, but only one Charlie!

CONCLUSION

Looking back at all the cowboy villains that flashed across the silver screen, King ranks among the most memorable. He certainly was a great badman, but he did work often, and his villainy became rather cuddly as the years progressed and as King added more and more weight. However, Charles King did make his mark on screen history, and he remains in the memories of those of us who shared so many pleasant Saturday

Don Barry has just given King a bellyache (DESERT BANDIT, Republic, 1941).

matinees watching him die a hundred screen death — deaths that he had so justly deserved.

So long Charlie, we loved to hate you.

Charlie seems disappointed that Bob Steele's boot won't fit him.

CHARLES KING'S SOUND FILMOGRAPHY

(Thanks to researcher/author/historian, Les Adams)

Date	Title	Co.	Star	King Role
8/8/30	OKLAHOMA CYCLONE	Tif	Bob Steele	McKim (Black Diablo)
10/1/30	BEYOND THE LAW	Ray	Robert Frazer	Brand
11/23/30	DAWN TRAIL, THE	Col	Buck Jones	Skeets
12/23/30	FIGHTIN' THRU	Tif	Ken Maynard	Fox Tyson
3/1/31	THE MYSTERY TROOPER (Serial)	Syn	Robert Frazer	Gang Leader Mack
5/15/31	THE TWO GUN MAN	Tif	Ken Maynard	Thorne
7/15/31	ALIAS THE BAD MAN	Tif	Ken Maynard	Black Mike Richards
9/13/31	ARIZONA TERROR	Tif	Ken Maynard	Henchman Ike
10/11/31	RANGE LAW	Tif	Ken Maynard	Bull Legal
11/8/31	BRANDED MEN	Tif	Ken Maynard	Mace
12/6/31	POCATELLO KID, THE	Tif	Ken Maynard	One-Eye Trinidad
1/2/32	GHOST CITY	Mon	Bill Cody	Buck
1/17/32	THE GAY BUCKAROO	All	Hoot Gibson	Faro Parker
3/7/32	HOTEL CONTINENTAL	Tif	Peggy Shannon	Bit
4/15/32	VANISHING MEN	Mon	Tom Tyler	Butch Grimes
6/11/32	A MAN'S LAND	All	Hoot Gibson	Joe
6/20/32	HONOR OF THE MOUNTED	Mon	Tom Tyler	Frenchy
8/5/32	CORNERED	Col	Tim McCoy	Cowhand
8/9/32	THE HURRICANE EXPRESS (Serial)	Mas	John Wayne	Henchman Mike
8/28/32	FIGHTING FOR JUSTICE	Col	Tim McCoy	Carson
10/1/32	OUTLAW JUSTICE	Maj	Jack Hoxie	Volger
10/16/32	BETWEEN FIGHTING MEN	WW	Ken Maynard	Cowhand

10/21/32 .. THE MAN FROM ARIZONA .. Mon .. Rex Bell .... Unknown

11/2/32 .. UNDER MONTANA SKIES . Tif ..... Kenneth Harlan ...... Frank Blake

11/15/32 .. YOUNG BLOOD .... Mon .. Bob Steele .... Sheriff Jack Sharpe

11/20/32 .. FARGO EXPRESS .... WW .. Ken Maynard .... Gambler chasing Mort

12/15/32 .. THE FIGHTING CHAMP ..... Mon .. Bob Steele .... Jock Malone

12/30/32 .. CRASHING BROADWAY .... Mon .. Rex Bell .... Gus Jeffries

4/6/33 .. DUDE BANDIT, THE .... All ..... Hoot Gibson .... Cowhand

5/5/33 .. SON OF THE BORDER ...... RKO . Tom Keene .... Henchley

5/14/33 .. LONE AVENGER, THE .... WW .. Ken Maynard .... Nip Hawks

5/29/33 .. FIGHTING PARSON, THE .. Alli.... Hoot Gibson .... Mike

10/26/33 .. STRAWBERRY ROAN .... Uni ... Ken Maynard .... Cowhand Curley

4/12/34 .. MYSTERY RANCH .... Rel .... Tom Tyler .... Henchman Sam

8/15/34 .. DEFENSE RESTS, THE ...... Col ... Jack Holt .... Reporter

9/1/34 .. LAW OF THE WILD (Serial) . Mas .. Bob Custer .... Henchman

9/25/34 .. INSIDE INFORMATION .... S&S .. Rex Lease .... Henchman

9/28/34 .. MEN IN BLACK (Short) ...... Col ... Three Stooges ...... Bit

10/6/34 .. LADY BY CHOICE .... Col ... Carole Lombard ...... The Drunk

11/1/34 .. PERFECTLY MISMATED (Short) Col ... Leon Errol .... Bit

11/8/34 .. PRESCOTT KID, THE .... Col ... Tim McCoy .... J. Bones

11/15/34 .. THE FIGHTING TROOPER . Amb . Kermit Maynard .... Landeau

11/23/34 .. JEALOUSY .... Col ... Nancy Carroll .... Bit

1/25/35 .. HIS OLD FLAME (Short) .... Col ... Roger Gray .... Bit

1/26/35 .. THE CROOKED TRAIL .... Sup .. Johnny Mack Brown . Lanning

2/1/35 .. NORTHERN FRONTIER ..... Amb . Kermit Maynard .... Constable Wallace

2/1/35 .. MILLION DOLLAR HAUL ... S&S . Reed Howes .... Henchman

2/15/35 .. LAW BEYOND THE RANGE . Col ... Tim McCoy .... Townsman

2/22/35 .. THE WHOLE TOWN'S TALKING . Col ... Edward G. Robinson . Bit

3/5/35 .. TAILSPIN TOMMY IN THE .. Uni ... Clark Williams .... Henchman
GREAT AIR MYSTERY (Serial)

3/18/35 .. THE REVENGE RIDER .... Col ... Tim McCoy .... Henchman

4/1/35 .. BORN TO BATTLE .... Rel .... Tom Tyler .... Jim Lommer

4/20/35 .. THE RED BLOOD OF COURAGE . Amb . Kermit Maynard .... Henchman Joe

5/1/35 .. AIR HAWKS .... Col ... Ralph Bellamy ...... Ambulance Driver

5/2/35 .. SILENT VALLEY .... Rel .... Tom Tyler .... Harry Keller

5/10/35 .. EIGHT BELLS .... Col ... Ann Sothern .... Chauffeur

5/11/35 .. SILVER BULLET, THE .... Rel .... Tom Tyler .... Luke Hargrove

5/18/35 .. THE MIRACLE RIDER (Serial) .. Mas .. Tom Mix .... Henchman Hatton

7/1/35 .. THE ROARING WEST (Serial) .. Uni ... Buck Jones .... Henchman Tex

7/29/35 .. OUTLAWED GUNS .... Uni ... Buck Jones .... Frank Davilla

8/1/35 .. SUNDOWN SAUNDERS ..... Sup .. Bob Steele .... Jack Mace

8/15/35 .. THE MAN FROM GUNTOWN . Pur ... Tim McCoy .... Henchman

8/31/35 .. THE ADVENTURES OF ...... Mas .. Kane Richmond ..... Henchman Martin
REX AND RINTY (Serial)

9/5/35 .. TUMBLING TUMBLEWEEDS . Re ..... Gene Autry .... Henchman Blaze

9/24/35 .. THE PUBLIC MENACE .... Col ... Jean Arthur .... Photographer

9/25/35 .. HIS FIGHTING BLOOD .... Amb . Kermit Maynard .... Constable Black

11/5/35 .. THE IVORY-HANDLED GUN Uni ... Buck Jones .... Henchman Tom

12/11/35 .. THE SINGING VAGABOND Rep .. Gene Autry .... Henchman Red

12/15/35 .. SWIFTY .... Div .... Hoot Gibson .... Poker Player

12/20/35 .. TRAIL OF TERROR .... Sup .. Bob Steele .... Hashknife

12/30/35 .. JUST MY LUCK .... Cor ... Charles Ray .... Unbilled

1/22/36 .. SUNSET OF POWER .... Uni ... Buck Jones .... Jim Coley

1/25/36 .. VALLEY OF THE LAWLESS . Supr . Johnny Mack Brown . Regan

2/5/36 .. THE KID RANGER .... Sup .. Bob Steele .... Joe

2/15/36 .. THE LAWLESS NINETIES .. Rep .. John Wayne .... Henchman Hartley

2/20/36 .. LUCKY TERROR .... Div .... Gibson .... Lawyer Wheeler

2/24/36 .. FAST BULLETS .... Rel .... Tom Tyler .... Henchman Bill

3/2/36 .. RED RIVER VALLEY .... Rep .. Gene Autry .... Henchman Sam

3/10/36 .. DESERT PHANTOM .... Sup .. Johnny Mack Brown . Henchman Dan

3/27/36 .. O'MALLEY OF THE MOUNTED Fox ... George O'Brien ..... Brody

5/10/36 .. LAST OF THE WARRENS .. Sup .. Bob Steele .... Kent

5/14/36 .. PINTO RUSTLERS .... Rel .... Tom Tyler .... Henchman Jim

5/21/36 .. BURNING GOLD .... Win ... William Boyd .... Henchman

5/25/36 .. THE LONELY TRAIL .... Rep .. John Wayne .... Sentry

6/22/36 .. GUNS AND GUITARS .... Rep .. Gene Autry .... Henchman Sam

6/25/36 .. THE LAW RIDES .... Sup .. Bob Steele .... Hank Davis

7/1/36 .. THE COWBOY AND THE KID . Uni ... Buck Jones .... Deputy

8/6/36 .. IDAHO KID .... CY .... Rex Bell .... Bibb Slagel

8/15/36 .. BRAND OF THE OUTLAWS .. Sup .. Bob Steele .... Rufe Matlock

8/15/36 .. SANTA FE BOUND .... Rel .... Tom Tyler .... Steve Denton

8/15/36 .. HEARTS IN BONDAGE ...... Rep .. Lew Ayres .... Bit

9/29/36 .. MEN OF THE PLAINS .... CY .... Rex Bell .... Johnson

10/10/36 .. SHADOW OF CHINATOWN .. Vic .... Bela Lugosi .... Henchman Grogan
(Serial)

10/15/36 .. RIP ROARIN' BUCKAROO . Vic .... Tom Tyler .... Bones Kennedy

11/28/36 ... THE PHANTOM OF THE RANGE . Vic .... Tom Tyler .... Henchman Tex

12/6/36 .. HATS OFF .... GN .... John Payne .... 'Handsome'

12/20/36 .. HEADIN' FOR THE RIO GRANDE . GN .... Tex Ritter .... Henchman Tick

12/25/36 .. HEADLINE CRASHER .... Amb . Frankie Darro .... Henchman Blake

2/15/37 .. THE GAMBLING TERROR . Rep .. Johnny Mack Brown . Brett

3/1/37 .. OLD LOUISIANA .... Cres . Tom Keene .... Guard

3/6/37 .. TROUBLE IN TEXAS .... GN .... Tex Ritter .... Henchman Pinto

3/24/37 .. LIGHTNIN' CRANDALL ...... Rep .. Bob Steele .... Carson Blaine

4/3/37 .. HITTIN' THE TRAIL .... GN .... Tex Ritter .... Henchman Slug

5/4/37 .. THE TRUSTED OUTLAW ... Rep .. Bob Steele .... Bert Gilmore

5/12/37 .. ROOTIN' TOOTIN' RHYTHM . Rep .. Gene Autry .... Jim Black

5/22/37 .. SING, COWBOY, SING .... GN .... Tex Ritter .... Henchman Red Holman

6/5/37 .. THE PAINTED STALLION .. Rep .. Ray Corrigan .... Bull Smith
(Serial)

6/6/37 .. SMOKE TREE RANGE .... Uni ... Buck Jones .... Henchman

6/21/37 .. A LAWMAN IS BORN .... Rep .. Johnny Mack Brown .. Henchman Bert Moscrip

7/2/37 .. RIDERS OF THE ROCKIES GN .... Tex Ritter .... Butch Regan

7/6/37 .. THE PHANTOM RIDER ...... Uni ... Buck Jones .... Henchman Keeler
(Serial)

7/19/37 .. THE RED ROPE .... Rep .. Bob Steele .... Red Mike

7/27/37 .. ISLAND CAPTIVES .... Fal .... Eddie Nugent .... Kelly

8/6/37 .. THE MYSTERY OF THE ..... GN .... Tex Ritter .... Blackie Devlin
HOODED HORSEMEN

9/2/37 .. GOD'S COUNTRY AND ...... Mon .. Tom Keene .... Red Gentry
.. THE MAN

9/5/37 .. BLACK ACES .... Uni ... Buck Jones .... Jess Walker

11/1/37 .. RIDIN' THE LONE TRAIL ... Rep .. Bob Steele .... Dusty Williams

11/3/37 .. DANGER VALLEY .... Mon .. Jack Randall .... Dana

11/17/37 .. LUCK OF ROARING CAMP . Mon .. Owen Davis, Jr. ..... Sandy

12/5/37 .. THE FIGHTING DEPUTY .... Spec . Fred Scott .... Scar Adams

1/21/38 .. TEX RIDES WITH THE BOY . GN .... Tex Ritter .... Bert Stark
.. SCOUTS

2/12/38 .. THE LONE RANGER (Serial) .. Rep .. Lee Powell .... Henchman Morley

3/4/38 .. FRONTIER TOWN .... GN .... Tex Ritter .... Pete Denby

3/7/38 .. THUNDER IN THE DESERT . Rep .. Bob Steele .... Curt Harris

4/1/38 .. SONGS AND BULLETS ...... Spec . Fred Scott .... Sheriff

5/1/38 .. FLAMING FRONTIERS .... Uni ... Johnny Mack Brown .. Henchman Blackie
.. (Serial)

5/29/38 .. PHANTOM RANGER .... Mon .. Tim McCoy .... Henchman Dan

6/1/38 .. SONGS AND SADDLES ..... RS/CY Gene Austin .... Falcon

6/6/38 .. MAN'S COUNTRY .... Mon .. Jack Randall .... Steve

7/5/38 .. GOLD MINE IN THE SKY ... Rep .. Gene Autry .... The Painter

7/8/38 .. PANAMINT'S BAD MAN ..... TCF .. Smith Ballew .... Henchman Hank

7/8/38 .. ROLLIN' PLAINS .... GN .... Tex Ritter .... Trigger Gargan

7/22/38 .. ON THE GREAT WHITE TRAIL . GN .... James Newill .... LaGrange

8/12/38 .. UTAH TRAIL .... GN .... Tex Ritter .... Henchman Badger

9/7/38 .. STARLIGHT OVER TEXAS . Mon .. Tex Ritter .... Hank Boston

10/19/38 .. WHERE THE BUFFALO ..... Mon .. Tex Ritter .... Henchman Bull
ROAM

Date	Title	Studio	Star	Role
11/2/38 ..	IN EARLY ARIZONA	Col ...	Bill Elliott	Kaintuck
11/15/38 ..	ADVENTURE IN SAHARA .	Col ...	Paul Kelly	Legionnaire
11/16/38 ..	GUN PACKER	Mon ..	Jack Randall	Chance Moore
11/18/38 ..	SANTA FE STAMPEDE	Rep ..	Three Mesquiteers .	Henchman Ben
12/7/38 ..	SONG OF THE BUCKAROO .	GN	Tex Ritter	Max Groat
12/21/38 ..	WILD HORSE CANYON	Mon ..	Jack Randall	Henchman Red
1/7/39 ..	THE PHANTOM CREEPS ... (Serial)	Uni ...	Bela Lugosi	Henchman Buck
1/13/39 ..	FRONTIERS OF '49	Col ...	Bill Elliott	Howard Brunton
1/15/39 ..	FEUD OF THE RANGE	Met ...	Bob Steele	Henchman Dirk
2/8/39 ..	SUNDOWN ON THE PRAIRIE .	Mon ..	Tex Ritter	Dorgan
3/1/39 ..	ROLLIN' WESTWARD	Mon ..	Tex Ritter	Haines
3/16/39 ..	LONE STAR PIONEERS	Col ...	Bill Elliott	Pike
4/12/39 ..	FRONTIER PONY EXPRESS .	Rep ..	Roy Rogers	Henchman
4/16/39 ..	THE LAW COMES TO TEXAS .	Col ...	Bill Elliott	Kaintuck
5/1/39 ..	THE OREGON TRAIL (Serial) .	Uni ...	Johnny Mack Brown ..	Henchman Dirk
5/10/39 ..	MESQUITE BUCKAROO	Met ...	Bob Steele	Trigger Carson
6/14/39 ..	DOWN THE WYOMING TRAIL .	Mon ..	Tex Ritter	George Becker
8/16/39 ..	RIDERS OF THE FRONTIER .	Mon ..	Tex Ritter	Henchman
10/10/39 ..	OKLAHOMA FRONTIER	Uni ...	Johnny Mack Brown ..	Soapy
10/12/39 ..	TAMING OF THE WEST	Col ...	Bill Elliott	Jackson
10/25/39 ..	MUTINY IN THE BIG HOUSE	Mon ..	Charles Bickford ..	Harris
11/29/39 ..	COWBOYS FROM TEXAS .	Rep ..	Three Mesquiteers ...	Henchman Bill
12/14/39 ..	DEATH RIDES THE RANGE	CY	Ken Maynard	Joe Larkin
12/15/39 ..	SOUTH OF THE BORDER .	Rep ..	Gene Autry	Bandit
12/16/39 ..	ZORRO'S FIGHTING LEGION (Serial)	Rep ..	Reed Hadley	Henchman Valdez
1/2/40 ..	THE SHADOW (Serial)	Col ...	Victor Jory	Henchman Russell
1/19/40 ..	WEST OF CARSON CITY ...	Uni ...	Johnny Mack Brown ..	Henchman Drag
2/20/40 ..	THE CHEYENNE KID	Mon ..	Jack Randall	Henchman Carson
3/30/40 ..	SON OF THE NAVY	Mon ..	James Dunn	Detective Duke Johnson
4/10/40 ..	HI-YO SILVER (Serial feature) .	Rep ..	Lee Powell	Henchman Morley
5/5/40 ..	TERRY AND THE PIRATES .. (Serial)	Col ...	Granville Owen	Henchman Blackie
6/1/40 ..	LIGHTNING STRIKES WEST .	Col ...	Ken Maynard	Larkin
6/26/40 ..	WILD HORSE RANGE	Mon ..	Jack Randall	Stoner
6/29/40 ..	ONE MAN'S LAW	Rep ..	Don Barry	Henchman Kells
7/19/40 ..	DEADWOOD DICK (Serial) .	Col ...	Don Douglas	Henchman Tex
9/30/40 ..	BILLY THE KID IN TEXAS ..	PRC ..	Bob Steele	Dave
9/30/40 ..	UNDER TEXAS SKIES	Rep ..	Three Mesquiteers ...	Rancher
10/1/40 ..	THE GREEN ARCHER .... (Serial)	Col ...	Victor Jory	Henchman Cardoni

12/12/40 .. PONY POST .... Uni ... Johnny Mack Brown .. Gambler Hamilton

12/27/40 .. BILLY THE KID'S GUN .... PRC .. Bob Steele .... Ed Baker
        JUSTICE

12/30/40 .. RIDERS FROM NOWHERE .. Mon .. Jack Randall .... Trigger

1/24/41 .. BILLY THE KID'S RANGE .. PRC .. Bob Steele .... Road Worker
        WAR

1/31/41 .. WHITE EAGLE (Serial) .... Col ... Buck Jones .... Henchman Brace

2/28/41 .. THE LONE RIDER CROSSES . PRC .. George Houston ... Jarvis (El Puma)
        THE RIO

3/7/41 .. OUTLAWS OF THE RIO ..... PRC .. Tim McCoy .... Trigger
        GRANDE

3/21/41 .. BURY ME NOT ON THE ..... Uni ... Johnny Mack Brown .. Townsman
        LONE PRAIRIE

4/18/41 .. BILLY THE KID'S FIGHTING .. PRC .. Bob Steele .... Badger
        PALS

4/18/41 .. ROAR OF THE PRESS .... Mon .. Wallace Ford .... Unbilled

5/16/41 .. THE LONE RIDER IN GHOST .. PRC .. George Houston ... Henchman Roberts
        TOWN

5/24/41 .. DESERT BANDIT .... Rep .. Don Barry .... Dying Henchman

Kermit Maynard, Charlie, Buster Crabbe and John Cason look serious while Fuzzy does his Indian imitation.

Date	Title	Studio	Star	Role
6/20/41	LAW OF THE RANGE	Uni	Johnny Mack Brown	Henchman Walt
7/11/41	BILLY THE KID IN SANTA FE	PRC	Bob Steele	Steve Barton
7/13/41	THE TEXAS MARSHAL	PRC	Tim McCoy	Ray Titus
8/15/41	THE IRON CLAW (Serial)	Col	Charles Quigley	Henchman Silk Landon
8/29/41	THE LONE RIDER AMBUSHED	PRC	George Houston	Ranch Hand
9/12/41	THE APACHE KID	Rep	Don Barry	Morgan
9/15/41	BADLANDS OF DAKOTA	Uni	Robert Stack	Plainview Gunman
9/19/41	THE GUNMAN FROM BODIE	Mon	Rough Riders	Henchman Steve
10/4/41	BILLY THE KID WANTED	PRC	Buster Crabbe	Jack Saunders
11/7/41	THE LONE RIDER FIGHTS BACK	PRC	George Houston	Henchman Mitter
12/5/41	LONE STAR LAW MEN	Mon	Tom Keene	Duke Lawson
12/5/41	BORROWED HERO	Mon	Alan Baxter	Unbilled
12/12/41	BILLY THE KID'S ROUND-UP	PRC	Buster Crabbe	Deputy Ed Slade
12/26/41	FORBIDDEN TRAILS	Mon	Rough Riders	Henchman Fulton
1/20/42	BELOW THE BORDER	Mon	Rough Riders	Steve Slade
2/20/42	RAIDERS OF THE WEST	PRC	Frontier Marshals	Duke Mallory
3/10/42	STAGECOACH EXPRESS	Rep	Don Barry	Bartender Talbot
3/27/42	GHOST TOWN LAW	Mon	Rough Riders	Henchman Gus
4/1/42	WHERE TRAILS END	Mon	Tom Keene	Jim Regan
4/24/42	BOOT HILL BANDITS	Mon	Range Busters	Henchman
5/29/42	PERILS OF THE ROYAL MOUNTED (Serial)	Col	Robert Stevens	Henchman
7/10/42	TUMBLEWEED TRAIL	PRC	Frontier Marshals	Vic Landreau
8/13/42	BAD MEN OF THE HILLS	Col	Charles Starrett	Attorney
8/21/42	LAW AND ORDER	PRC	Buster Crabbe	Mil Crawford
8/21/42	RIDERS OF THE WEST	Mon	Rough Riders	Henchman Hogan
9/4/42	ARIZONA STAGECOACH	Mon	Range Busters	Tim Douglas
9/4/42	PRAIRIE PALS	PRC	Frontier Marshals	Henchman Mitchell
9/28/42	BORDER ROUNDUP	PRC	George Houston	Henchman Blackie
10/2/42	SHERIFF OF SAGE VALLEY	PRC	Buster Crabbe	Sloane
10/14/42	ALONG THE SUNDOWN TRAIL	PRC	Frontier Marshals	Big Ben Salter
11/20/42	PIRATES OF THE PRAIRIE	RKO	Tim Holt	Vigilante Layton
11/28/42	OUTLAWS OF BOULDER PASS	PRC	George Houston	Henchman Jake
12/4/42	TRAIL RIDERS	Mon	Range Busters	Ed Cole
12/11/42	OVERLAND STAGECOACH	PRC	Bob Livingston	Henchman Jake
12/25/42	THE RANGERS TAKE OVER	PRC	Texas Rangers	Kip Lane
1/8/43	TWO FISTED JUSTICE	Mon	Range Busters	Trigger Farley
1/27/43	THE KID RIDES AGAIN	PRC	Buster Crabbe	Henchman Vic

2/19/43 .. HAUNTED RANCH .... Mon .. Range Busters ...... Henchman Chuck

3/5/43 .. BAD MEN OF THUNDER GAP . PRC .. Texas Rangers ...... Pete Holman

3/26/43 .. LAND OF HUNTED MEN .... Mon .. Range Busters ...... Faro Wilson

4/2/43 .. THE GHOST RIDER .... Mon .. Johnny Mack Brown . Steve Cook

4/9/43 .. KING OF THE COWBOYS .. Rep .. Roy Rogers .... Henchman

4/30/43 .. CALLING WILD BILL ELLIOTT . Rep .. Bill Elliott .... Ace

5/10/43 .. WEST OF TEXAS .... PRC .. Texas Rangers ...... Henchman

5/14/43 .. WESTERN CYCLONE .... PRC .. Buster Crabbe ...... Ace Harmon

5/21/43 .. RIDERS OF THE RIO .... Rep .. Three Mesquiteers . Thumper Cherokee
GRANDE

5/25/43 .. THE DESPERADOES .... Col ... Randolph Scott ..... Barfly

6/11/43 .. THE MAN FROM THUNDER . Rep .. Bill Elliott .... Peters
RIVER

6/15/43 .. BORDER BUCKAROOS ..... PRC .. Texas Rangers ...... Rance Daggert

7/8/43 .. BORDERTOWN .... Rep .. Bill Elliott .... Sheriff Barnes
GUN FIGHTERS

7/16/43 .. THE STRANGER FROM ..... Mon .. Johnny Mack Brown .. Henchman Harmond
PECOS

8/8/43 .. FIGHTING VALLEY .... PRC .. Texas Rangers ...... Henchman Slim

8/16/43 .. CATTLE STAMPEDE .... PRC .. Buster Crabbe ...... Brandon

8/23/43 .. DANGER! WOMEN AT .... PRC .. Mary Brian .... Policeman
WORK

9/4/43 .. BLAZING FRONTIER .... PRC .. Buster Crabbe ...... Sam

9/30/43 .. RAIDERS OF RED GAP ..... PRC .. Bob Livingston ..... Jack Bennett

10/8/43 .. BLAZING GUNS .... Mon .. Trail Blazers .... Blackie

10/15/43 .. OUTLAWS OF STAMPEDE .. Mon .. Johnny Mack Brown .. Henchman Steve
PASS

10/26/43 .. RETURN OF RANGERS ..... PRC .. Texas Rangers ...... Bill Thorne

11/5/43 .. THE DEVIL RIDERS .... PRC .. Buster Crabbe ...... Del Stone

11/20/43 .. BOSS OF RAWHIDE .... PRC .. Texas Rangers ...... Frank Hade

11/26/43 .. TEXAS KID, THE .... Mon .. Johnny Mack Brown .. Red Grogan

12/3/43 .. DEATH VALLEY RANGERS .. Mon .. Trail Blazers .... BLACKIE

12/23/43 .. COWBOY IN THE CLOUDS .. Col ... Charles Starrett .... Tripp

12/29/43 .. CALIFORNIA JOE .... Rep .. Don Barry .... Jim Ashley

3/4/44 .. FRONTIER OUTLAWS .... PRC .. Buster Crabbe ...... Barlow

3/18/44 .. ARIZONA WHIRLWIND ...... Mon .. Trail Blazers .... Duke Rollins

3/25/44 .. THUNDERING GUNSLINGERS . PRC .. Buster Crabbe ...... Steve Kirby

3/31/44 .. GUNS OF THE LAW .... PRC .. Texas Rangers ...... Kendall Lowther

4/18/44 .. OUTLAW TRAIL .... Mon .. Trail Blazers .... Chuck Walters

4/27/44 .. THE PINTO BANDIT .... PRC .. Texas Rangers ...... Henchman Spur Sneely

5/5/44 .. VALLEY OF VENGEANCE . PRC .. Buster Crabbe ...... Burke

6/3/44 .. SPOOK TOWN .... PRC .. Texas Rangers ...... Trigger Booth

Date	Title	Studio	Star	Character
6/10/44	SONORA STAGECOACH	Mon	Trail Blazers	BLACKIE REED
6/25/44	FUZZY SETTLES DOWN	PRC	Buster Crabbe	Lafe Barlow
7/1/44	HARMONY TRAIL (White Stallion)	Mat	Ken Maynard	Jim Sherrill
7/2/44	MARSHAL OF RENO	Rep	Bill Elliott	Stage Bandit
7/10/44	OUTLAW ROUNDUP	PRC	Texas Rangers	Frank Harkins
7/30/44	BRAND OF THE DEVIL	PRC	Texas Rangers	Bucko Lynn
9/2/44	RUSTLER'S HIDEOUT	PRC	Buster Crabbe	Buck Shaw
9/16/44	LAND OF THE OUTLAWS	Mon	Johnny Mack Brown	Bart Green
9/21/44	GANGSTERS OF THE FRONTIER	PRC	Texas Rangers	Henchman Haner
10/6/44	CODE OF THE PRAIRIE	Rep	Sunset Carson	Election Informer
10/28/44	WILD HORSE PHANTOM	PRC	Buster Crabbe	Henchman
11/4/44	LAW OF THE VALLEY	Mon	Johnny Mack Brown	Miller
11/9/44	DEAD OR ALIVE	PRC	Texas Rangers	Red Avery
11/15/44	THE GREAT MIKE	PRC	Buzzy Henry	Doc Slagel
12/9/44	OATH OF VENGEANCE	PRC	Buster Crabbe	Henchman Mort
12/23/44	ALASKA	Mon	Kent Taylor	Miner
12/30/44	THE BIG BONANZA	Rep	Richard Arlen	Big Ben
1/15/45	THE NAVAJO TRAIL	Mon	Johnny Mack Brown	Henchman Red
2/3/45	HIS BROTHER'S GHOST	PRC	Buster Crabbe	Thorne
2/8/45	MARKED FOR MURDER	PRC	Texas Rangers	Pete Magoo
4/1/45	FRONTIER FUGITIVES	PRC	Texas Rangers	Henchman
4/19/45	SHADOWS OF DEATH	PRC	Buster Crabbe	Steve Landreau
4/20/45	THE MONSTER AND THE APE (Serial)	Col	Robert Lowery	Policeman
5/7/45	ENEMY OF THE LAW	PRC	Texas Rangers	Charley Gray
5/16/45	THE LADY CONFESSES	PRC	Mary Beth Hughes	Policeman
5/17/45	BOTH BARRELS BLAZING	Col	Charles Starrett	Henchman Nevada
6/14/45	GANGSTER'S DEN	PRC	Buster Crabbe	Butch
7/12/45	THE WHITE GORILLA	WM	Ray Corrigan	Morgan
7/26/45	THREE IN THE SADDLE	PRC	Texas Rangers	Bert Rawlins
9/10/45	BORDER BADMEN	PRC	Buster Crabbe	Merritt
9/14/45	JUNGLE RAIDERS (Serial)	Col	Kane Richmond	Jake Raynes
10/15/45	FLAMING BULLETS	PRC	Texas Rangers	Porky Smith
10/21/45	FIGHTING BILL CARSON	PRC	Buster Crabbe	Henchman
11/21/45	THE NAVAJO KID	PRC	Bob Steele	Lee Hedges
11/25/45	FRONTIER FEUD	Mon	Johnny Mack Brown	Henchman
12/8/45	THE LONESOME TRAIL	Mon	Jimmy Wakely	Rancher
12/13/45	WHO'S GUILTY? (Serial)	Col	Robert Kent	Burk
2/17/46	AMBUSH TRAIL	PRC	Bob Steele	Al Craig

This time Bob Steele has the drop on Charlie. Check out Steele's boots.

4/12/46 .. THUNDER TOWN .... PRC .. Bob Steele .... Bill Rankin

4/20/46 .. THE CARAVAN TRAIL .... PRC .. Eddie Dean .... Joe King

6/30/46 .. COLORADO SERENADE ... PRC .. Eddie Dean .... Ranch Hand Muscles

6/30/46 .. GHOST OF HIDDEN VALLEY .. PRC .. Buster Crabbe ...... Ed 'Blackie' Dawson

7/11/46 .. CHICK CARTER, DETECTIVE . Col ... Lyle Talbot .... Joe Carney
　　　　 (Serial)

7/17/46 .. PRAIRIE BADMEN .... PRC .. Buster Crabbe ...... Cal

7/24/46 .. QUEEN OF BURLESQUE .. PRC .. Evelyn Ankers ...... Dugan

8/16/46 .. LAWLESS BREED .... Uni ... Kirby Grant .... Tim Carson

9/22/46 .. OUTLAWS OF THE PLAINS . PRC .. Buster Crabbe ...... Nord Finner

10/24/46 .. SON OF THE GUARDSMAN Col ... Robert Shaw .... Sir Edgar Bullard
　　　　 (Serial) ....

1/18/47 .. SON OF ZORRO (Serial) .... Rep .. George Turner ...... Dow

2/28/47 .. LAW OF THE LASH .... PRC .. Lash LaRue .... Sheriff

3/24/47 .. JESSE JAMES RIDES .... Rep .. Clayton Moore ...... Trent
　　　　 AGAIN (Serial)

4/5/47 .. THREE ON A TICKET .... PRC .. Hugh Beaumont ... A Drunk

5/31/47 .. KILLER AT LARGE .... PRC .. Robert Lowery ...... Bartender

7/28/47 .. WYOMING .... Rep .. Bill Elliott............... Homesteader

Date	Title	Studio	Star	Role
10/4/47 ..	RIDIN' DOWN THE TRAIL ..	Mon ..	Jimmy Wakely	Brown
11/1/47 ..	THE WISTFUL WIDOW OF . WAGON GAP	Uni ...	Abbott & Costello .	Henchman
11/20/47 ..	LAST DAYS OF BOOT HILL .	Col ...	Charles Starrett	Henchman Nevada
12/18/47 ..	BRICK BRADFORD (Serial) .	Col ...	Kane Richmond	Henchman Creed
1/5/48 ..	SUPERMAN (Serial)	Col ...	Kirk Alyn	Conrad
3/28/48 ..	OKLAHOMA BLUES	Mon ..	Jimmy Wakely	Henchman Gabe
4/1/48 ..	TEX GRANGER (Serial)	Col ...	Robert Kellard	Henchman
4/10/48 ..	THE HAWK OF POWDER .. RIVER	PRC ..	Eddie Dean	Henchman
10/28/48 ..	CONGO BILL (Serial)	Col ...	Don McGuire	Kleeg
2/10/49 ..	BRUCE GENTRY (Serial) ...	Col ...	Tom Neal	Henchman Ivor
5/1/49 ..	STAMPEDE	AA	Rod Cameron	Ed
6/30/49 ..	GHOST OF ZORRO (Serial) ..	Rep ..	Clayton Moore	Henchman Joe
12/22/49 ..	ADVENTURES OF SIR .... GALAHAD (Serial)	Col ...	George Reeves	Sir Boris
4/17/50 ..	WESTERN PACIFIC AGENT .	Lip	Kent Taylor	Vagrant
7/20/50 ..	ATOM MAN VS. SUPERMAN . (Serial)	Col ...	Kirk Alyn	Henchman & Blackmailer
8/12/50 ..	GUNFIRE	Lip	Don Barry	Gunman
1/1/53 ..	THE GREAT ADVENTURES OF CAPTAIN KIDD (Serial)	Col ...	Richard Crane	Andrews

Fuzzy St. John takes on Charlie, while Buster Crbbe beats up Glenn Strange (CATTLE STAMPEDE, PRC, 1945).

KING'S SILENT FEATURES

1921.... SINGING RIVER
1921.... MOTION TO ADJOURN
1922.... PRICE OF YOUTH
1922.... BLACK BAG
1922.... MERRY-GO-ROUND
1925.... TRIPLE ACTION
1925.... SOMEWHERE IN WRONG
1927.... RANGE COURAGE
1928.... YOU CAN'T BEAT THE LAW
1928.... SISTERS OF EVE
1929.... SLIM FINGERS

The films listed above are in addition to the "Ike and Mike" short comedies, and I feel sure it is a partial list of Charlie's silent work. King may have also appeared as an extra in the 1915 film THE BIRTH OF A NATION. He can also be spotted in lots of films where stock footage was used.

INDEX OF FILM COMPANIES:

AA	Allied
ALLI	Allied Artists
COL	Columbia
COR	Corona
CRE	Crescent
CY	Colony
DIV	Diversion
FAL	Falcon
GN	Grand National
LIP	Lippert
MAJ	Majestic
MAS	Mascot
MAT	Mattox
MET	Metropolitan
MON	Monogram
PRC	Producers Releasing Corporation
PUR	Puritan
RAY	Raytone
REL	Reliable
REP	Republic
RS/CY	Road Show/Colony
SPEC	Spectrum
SUP	Supreme
S & S	Stage and Screen
SYN	Syndicate
TCF	20th Centruy Fox
TIF	Tiffany
UNI	Universal
VIC	Victory
WIN	Winchester
WM	Weiss-Merrick
WW	World Wide

PHOTO GALLERY

King as "Sir Edgar Bullard" in the serial, SON OF THE GUARDSMAN (Columbia, 1946).

We learn that clothes do not make the man.

Charlie better get his hands off the damsel (Suzanne Kaaren) before Tim McCoy lets him have it (PHANTOM RANGER, Monogram, 1938).

Once again, King has the drop on Bob Steele. Charlie plays "Rufe" (BRAND OF THE OUTLAWS, Supreme, 1936).

King has the drop on Ken Maynard while Frank Wayne, Bob Terry, and Reed Howes lend support.

Tim McCoy demonstrates his steely-eyed stare to Charlie (PHANTOM RANGER, Monogram, 1938).

Gene Autry takes old, ugly George Chesebro for a spin while Smiley Burnette tries to prevent King from joining the fracas.

Hats Off TO THE

B A D

M A N

for making our heroes the heroes.

King and some other badmen. Top row left to right: Harry Woods, Bob Kortman, I. Stanford Jolley, Tris Coffin. Middle row left to right: Kenneth MacDonald, Charles King, John Merton, Ted Adams. Bottom row left to right: Bud Geary, Terry Frost, Bob Wilke, Roy Barcroft.

King gets the upper hand on Lee Powell. That's Art Davis on the floor, and Bill "Cowboy Rambler" Boyd behind Davis (PRAIRIE PALS, PRC, 1942).

James Newill and Dave O'Brien have things their way (BRAND OF THE DEVIL, PRC, 1944)

Marshall Reed has things under control as King, Kermit Maynard, Stanley Price, Ed Cobb, and others look on (THE TEXAS KID, Monogram, 1943).

Hal Price, King, and John Merton, give instructions to old-timer, John Elliott (FUZZY SETTLES DOWN, PRC, 1944).

This time it's Tom Keene beating up on Charlie.

Roy Barcroft, King, Black Jack O'Shea, and Harry Worth (RIDERS OF
THE RIO GRANDE, Republic, 1943).

King as "Kleeg" in the cliffhanger, CONGO BILL (Columbia, 1948).

Charlie is plotting more mischief.

Emmett Lynn and Charlie in the Buster Crabbe starring film, GANGSTER'S DEN, (PRC, 1945).

8

King, Eddie Dean, Lee Powell, and Glenn Strange.

Black Jack O'Shea, Lash LaRue, King, Eddie Dean, and Emmett Lynn.

Kermit Maynard, Buster Crabbe, Frank Ellis, and King.

Bob Steele, and the alarm clock are about to awaken King (THE LAST OF THE WARRENS, Supreme, 1936.)

"You've got company," says Buster Crabbe (SHADOWS OF DEATH, PRC, 1945).

Dave Sharpe takes on King while Rex Bell handles another thug.

ABOUT THE AUTHOR

Reared in Oak Ridge, Tennessee, Bobby Copeland began going to the Saturday matinee B-Western movies at nearby theaters. He was immediately impressed by the moral code of these films, and has tried to pattern his life after the example set by the cowboy heroes. After graduating from high school and attending Carson-Newman College and the University of Tennessee, he set out to raise a family and start a career at the Oak Ridge National Laboratory. His love for the old Western films was put on the shelf and lay dormant for some 35 years. One Saturday, in the mid-eighties, he happened to turn on his television and the station was showing a Lash LaRue picture. This rekindled his interest. He contacted the TV program's host ("Marshal" Andy Smalls), and was invited to appear on the program. Since that time, Bobby has had some 100 articles published, contributed to twelve books, made several speeches, appeared on television over 20 times, and has been interviewed by several newspapers and four independent radio stations, as well as the Public Radio Broadcasting System to provide commentary and promote interest in B-Western films. In 1985 he was a co-founder of the Knoxville, Tennessee-based "Riders of the Silver Screen Club," serving five times as president. He initiated and continues to edit the club's newsletter. In 1996, his first book *Trail Talk* was published by Empire Publishing, Inc. (one of the world's largest publishers of books on Western films and performers) It was followed by *B-Western Boot Hill, Bill Elliott: The Peaceable Man, Roy Barcroft: King of the Badmen,* and *Silent Hoofbeats.* In addition to these popular books, Bobby also self-published *The Bob Baker Story, The Whip Wilson Story,* and *Five Heroes.* He has attended some 45 Western film festivals, and met many of the Western movie performers. He continues to contribute articles to the various Western magazines, and he is a regular columnist for *Western Clippings.* In 1988, Bobby received the "Buck Jones Rangers Trophy," presented annually to individuals demonstrating consistent dedication to keeping the spirit of the B-Western alive. In 1994, Don Key (Empire Publishing) and Boyd Magers (Video West, Inc. & *Western Clippings*) awarded Bobby the "Buck Rainey Shoot-em-Ups Pioneer Award," which yearly honors a fan who has made significant contributions towards the preservation of interest in the B-Westerns.

Bobby is a deacon, Sunday School teacher and an usher at Oak Ridge's Central Baptist Church. He retired in 1996 after 40 years at the same workplace. Bobby plans to continue his church work, write more B-Western articles, and enjoy his retirement with his faithful sidekick, Joan.

Bobby Copeland

104

More Great Books by Bobby Copeland...

B-WESTERN BOOT HILL
A Final Tribute to the Cowboys and Cowgirls
Who Rode the Saturday Matinee Movie Range

by Bobby j. Copeland

NEWLY REVISED AND UPDATED! Now includes the obituaries of Rex Allen, Dale Evans, Walter Reed, Clayton Moore, and others. *You asked for it—now here it is ... an extensively updated version of B-WESTERN BOOT HILL. (The first printing sold out!) An easy reference guide with hundreds of new entries, updates, and revisions. If you've worn out your original BOOT HILL, or are looking for a more complete B-Western reference book, this is the book for you!*

* 1000+ ENTRIES *
The Most Complete List Ever Assembled of Birth Dates, Death Dates, and Real Names of Those Beloved B-Western Performers.

* IT'S A LITERARY MILESTONE *
Bobby Copeland has produced a literary milestone which surely will rank at the top among those important Western film history books printed within the past 30 years. *Richard B. Smith, III*

* OBITUARIES AND BURIAL LOCATIONS *
Through the years, Bobby Copeland has collected actual obituaries of hundreds of B-Western heroes, heavies, helpers, heroines and side-kicks. Also included is a listing of actual burial locations of many of the stars.

$15.00
(+ $2.00 s/h)

* MANY PHOTOS THROUGHOUT *

- -

TRAIL TALK
by Bobby J. Copeland

* IT'S A WESTERN STAR QUOTE BOOK *
Hundreds and Hundreds of Quotes from Your Favorite Cowboys and Cowgirls.

IT'S A WESTERN MOVIE TRIVIA BOOK
You Will Learn...
• What member of TV's "Gunsmoke" was Rex Allen's cousin.
• Who told the studio that the Lone Ranger role was stupid.
• What famous cowboy star divorced his wife and married his mother-in-law.
• Much, much more!

* IT'S A WESTERN MOVIE HISTORY BOOK *
• It informs who were the top 10 money makers from 1936-1954.
• The real names of Cowboys & Cowgirls.
• What America meant to John Wayne
• And more!

ONLY $12.50
(+ $2.00 s/h)

EMPIRE PUBLISHING, INC. • PO BOX 717 • MADISON, NC 27025

SILENT HOOFBEATS

by Bobby J. Copeland

A Salute to the Horses and Riders of the Bygone B-Western Era

A beautiful book saluting the great and beautiful horses of the Saturday matinee Westerns! They are all here—Trigger, Champion, Black Jack, Topper and all the rest. Not only is this a book about the horses, but it also contains extensive commentary by the cowboy heroes. And, it is loaded with wonderful photographs.

You will learn many of horses' backgrounds, how they were obtained by the cowboys, and incidents and accidents that happened while filming.

You will also learn which cowboy
...broke his arm when he fell from his horse and had to be replaced by another star.
...cried when his horse died.
...said horses were stupid
...beat his horses until they screamed.
...had his horse buried, instead of stuffed, because it was cheaper.
Plus...many more interesting and revealing items.

Bobby Copeland has become a well-versed Western writer in recent years. His down-to-earth style appeals to most every fan.

$20.00
(+ $2.00 s/h)

ROY BARCROFT: King of the Badmen

by Bobby J. Copeland

A WONDERFUL BOOK ABOUT A GREAT CHARACTER ACTOR

In this book, you will find:
• A detailed biography
• Foreword by Monte Hale
• How he selected the name "Roy Barcroft"
• Letters and comments by Roy
• Roy's views about his co-workers
• Co-workers' comments about Roy
• Roy's fans speak out
• Other writers' opinions of Roy Barcraft
• Filmography

$15.00
(+ $2.00 s/h)

BILL ELLIOTT: The Peaceable Man

by Bobby J. Copeland

* UNLIKE ANYTHING EVER PRODUCED ON BILL ELLIOTT *

• Wild Bill Elliott
• Bill Elliott in the Comics
• Bill Elliott's Personal Life
• Popularity Ranking of Bill Elliott
• Bill Elliott's Obituary
• They Knew Bill Elliott
• Bill Elliott's Principal Sidekicks
• Bill Elliott and His Horses
• The Real Wild Bill vs. The Reel Wild Bills
• They're Talking about Bill Elliott
• The Starring and Non-Starring Films of Bill Elliott

$15.00
(+ $2.00 s/h)

EMPIRE PUBLISHING, INC. • PO BOX 717 • MADISON, NC 27025

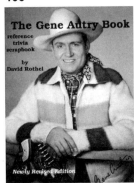

THE
GENE AUTRY
Reference-Trivia-Scrapbook
BOOK
by David Rothel

HERE IS EVERYTHING YOU EVER WANTED TO KNOW ABOUT AMERICA'S FAVORITE SINGING COWBOY, GENE AUTRY!

• **One Man's Life—Another Man's Trivia.** A giant, comprehensive compendium of questions and answers—little-known facts about a well-known cowboy.

• **The Wit and Wisdom of Gene Autry**. Memorable quotes on a wide range of subjects.

• **The Films of Gene Autry.** A complete Filmography!

• **Gene Autry on Tour.** Gene, Champion, and a whole entourage of entertainers played as many as 85 dates on a single tour. The stories they have to tell!

• **Gene Autry—On the Record**. A complete discography!

• **"The Gene Autry Show" TV Series.** This is the FIRST publication of the credits for Gene Autry's TV Series—ALL 91 episodes!

• **"Melody Ranch Theater."** During the 1980s, Gene was back on TV hosting his classic Western films.

• **The Autry Museum of Western Heritage**—Gene's long-time dream comes true!

ALL OF THIS AND MUCH MORE! $25.00 (+ $3.00 shipping/handling)

HERE IS EVERYTHING YOU EVER WANTED TO KNOW ABOUT "THE KING OF THE COWBOYS," ROY ROGERS!

THE
ROY ROGERS
Reference-Trivia-Scrapbook
BOOK
by David Rothel

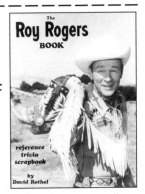

• **A conversation with The King of the Cowboys.**

• **One Man's Life—Another Man's Trivia.** A giant, comprehensive compendium of questions and answers—little-known facts about a well-known cowboy.

• **The Films of Roy Rogers.** A complete filmography!

• **Roy Rogers—On the Record.** A complete discography!

• **"The Roy Rogers Show" TV Series.** This is the FIRST publication of the credits for Roy's TV series—all 100 episodes!

• **A Roy Rogers Scrapbook of Clippings.** Rare fan magazine reprints of Roy Rogers articles!

• **Collecting Roy Rogers Memorabilia.** From lunchboxes to cap pistols, you'll see photos and current values of these hard-to-find collectibles.

ALL OF THIS AND MUCH MORE! $25.00 (+ $3.00 shipping/handling)

EMPIRE PUBLISHING, INC. • PO BOX 717 • MADISON, NC 27025

Richard Boone

"A Knight without Armor in a Savage Land"
by David Rothel

- MILESTONES AND MINUTIAE
- IN-DEPTH INTERVIEWS WITH FAMILY MEMBERS
- IN-DEPTH INTERVIEWS WITH FRIENDS AND CO-WORKERS:
- THE WIT AND WISDOM OF RICHARD BOONE.
- *MEDIC* Episode Guide.
- *HAVE GUN, WILL TRAVEL* Episode Guide.
- *THE RICHARD BOONE SHOW* Episode Guide.
- *HEC RAMSEY* Episode Guide.
- TV MOVIES & ANTHOLOGY TV PROGRAMS Episode Guide.

Each copy of *RICHARD BOONE, "A Knight without Armor in a Savage Land"* is packaged (at no extra cost) with a Johnny Western CD featuring "The Ballad of Paladin" and "The Guns of Rio Muerto," the only commercial recording Richard Boone made.

FREE Johnny Western CD

ORDER YOUR COPY NOW!
only **$30.00** postpaid for softcover
Includes *FREE* Johnny Western CD

Author David Rothel is a Western film historian who has also written An Ambush of Ghosts, Tim Holt, and Richard Boone, A Knight Without Armor in a Savage Land, among several other titles.

Those Great
COWBOY SIDEKICKS
by David Rothel

- 8-1/2 x 11
- 300+ PAGES
- BEAUTIFUL COLOR COVER
- OVER 200 PHOTOS
- **$25.00** (+ $3.00 s/h)

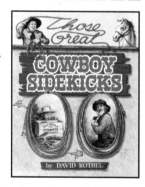

This book features in-depth profiles of such fondly-remembered character actors as George "Gabby" Hayes, Smiley Burnette, Andy Devine, Al "Fuzzy" St. John, Pat Buttram, Max Terhune, Fuzzy Knight, and many other sidekicks of the B-Westerns—thirty-nine in all! Much of *Those Great Cowboy Sidekicks* is told through the reminiscences of the sidekicks themselves and the cowboy stars who enjoyed the company of these often bewhiskered, tobacco-chewing saddle pals. Mr. Rothel provides the reader with the rare opportunity to go behind the scenes to discover the manner in which Western screen comedy was created.

EMPIRE PUBLISHING, INC. • PO BOX 717 • MADISON, NC 27025

THE **ROUND-UP**
by Donald R. Key

As time marches on, and so many of our screen and personal friends leave us, books like *The Round-Up* become even more important to us and to the history of Westerns.
—*Neil Summers*

Relive those treasured Saturday afternoons of your youth when you cheered on your favorite B-Western cowboy heroes; Tom Mix, Hoot Gibson, Ken Maynard, Tim McCoy, Gene Autry, Dale Evans, Roy Rogers, Lash LaRue, the Durango Kid, Buck Jones, Hopalong Cassidy, Wild Bill Elliott, Sunset Carson. And bring back memories of the Classic TV-Western cowboys and the more recent A-Western stars.

They're all here in what may be the most comprehensive (and attractive) Western star picture book ever produced. You get 298 heroes, heroines, stuntmen, sidekicks, villains, and cattlepunchers, plus 2 musical groups (the Cass County Boys and the Sons of the Pioneers).

From old-time stuntman Art Acord to Tony Young (who played Cord in TV's *Gunslinger),* from Harry Carey to Clint Eastwood, this handsome volume includes all your favorites from the turn of the century through the 1990s, arranged in alphabetical order for easy reference.

But this is more than just a pictorial. Each full-page entry includes a discretely placed one-paragraph background summary of the actor of group, with dates of birth and death. PLUS you get all these EXTRAS:

$27⁰⁰
(+ $3⁰⁰ s/h)

- Revised Edition
- Foreword by Monte Hale
- Afterword by Neil Summers
- Bibliography
- Quality hardcover to withstand repeated use.

- 200 pages
- Full color cover
- More than 100 photos
- $18.00 (+$2.00 shipping)

MORE COWBOY
SHOOTING STARS
by
John A. Rutherford
and
Richard B. Smith, III

$18⁰⁰
(+ $2.00 s/h)

This is a hardcover reference book that contains almost every Western film produced from 1930 through 1992 — The B's, The A's — they all are included. This reference book has each Western film star listed with each of their films in chronological order. There are 7,267 entries in all with 105 cowboy and cowgirl pictures are within.

Hardcover; 214 pages.

EMPIRE PUBLISHING, INC. • PO BOX 717 • MADISON, NC 27025

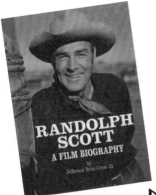

RANDOLPH SCOTT
A FILM BIOGRAPHY

by Jefferson Brim Crow, III

This book contains the only complete biography of this legendary star.

$**25**^{00}$
(+ 3^{00} s/h)

- 8-1/2 x 11
- Beautiful color cover
- Over 250 photographs
- 302 pages
- Softcover

WHATEVER HAPPENED TO RANDOLPH SCOTT?

by C. H. Scott

This is not just another book about a movie actor who made it to the glamour and glitz of the Hollywood scene. It is a love story that reveals the respect and admiration of a son for his father. Upon reading this narrative, one will experience growing up in the home of Randolph Scott, through the eyes of his son, Chris. As the reader begins to grieve the loss of one of Hollywood's finest stars, the answer to the question, *Whatever Happened to Randolph Scott?* will fill the heart with hope . . . he lives on in those who loved him. Includes many rare, personal photos.

$**12.95**
(+ 2^{00} shipping)

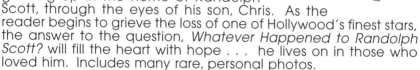

EMPIRE PUBLISHING, INC. • PO BOX 717 • MADISON, NC 27025

By SUE GOSSETT

THE FILMS AND CAREER OF
AUDIE MURPHY

by Sue Gossett

A Film-by-film Synopses of this
Legendary Hollywood Star / War Hero

This book reflects all of Audie Murphy's movie career of 44 films. Also included are two of his three made-for-television movies and one episode of his 1961 series, "Whispering Smith."

Along with acting and producing films, Audie's brilliant and well-documented war record is highlighted for those who want a thumb-nail account of what he endured while in the service of his country. This young man was not yet old enough to vote when he was awarded every combat medal for valor this nation had to offer.

Audie Murphy loved country music and expressed himself through the lyrics of dozens of songs, some of which were recorded by famous artists. Some of his poetry and songs are included in a special chapter. Order today!

$18.00

(+ $3⁰⁰ shipping)

$30⁰⁰

+ $3.00 shipping

Audie Murphy:
NOW SHOWING

by Sue Gossett

Audie Murphy

NOW SHOWING

by Sue Gossett

To celebrate the movie career of Audie Murphy, Sue Gossett and Empire Publishing are delighted to present this volume of *Audie Murphy: Now Showing*. It contains 200+ pages and more than 500 photo illustrations of advertising materials used to promote the 44 films given to Audie's credit. The contents include photos of movie 1-sheet posters, lobby and window display cards, half sheets, publicity items, author's comments, and more. *A must-have for the true Audie Murphy fan!*

Contents include:

- The movie magic of this legendary giant as illustrated via theatrical promotional materials.
- 200+ pages
- More than 500 photo illustrations
- Complete filmography
- Foreign items and testimonials
- Interviews with actors who appeared in his films
- Locations where movies were filmed
- Brief synopsis of each film
- Much more!

Author Sue Gossett is a true Audie Murphy historian, having followed his career since 1954.

EMPIRE PUBLISHING INC.

EMPIRE PUBLISHING, INC. • PO BOX 717 • MADISON, NC 27025

SINGING
in the SADDLE
The History of the Singing Cowboy
by Douglas B. Green

A singing cowboy himself, Douglas B. Green (better known as Ranger Doug from the Grammy Award-winning group Riders in the Sky) is uniquely suited to write the story of the singing cowboy. He has been collecting information an interviews on western music, films, and performers for nearly thirty years. In this volume, he traces this history from the early days of vaudeville and radio, through the heyday of movie westerns before World War II, to the current revival. He provides rich and careful analysis of the studio system that made men such as Gene Autry and Roy Rogers famous and he documents the role that country music and regional television stations played in carrying on the singing cowboy tradition after World War II. Through his close friendships with other singing cowboys and their families, Green is able to provide rare insights into the ways that some, like Autry, became stars while others did not.

- **Hardcover with beautiful color dust jacket**
- **Almost 400 pages on glossy stock**
- **Lots of photos, many rare**

$34.95
(+ $3⁰⁰ shipping)

"Tumbling Tumbleweeds" and "Cool Water" are only a couple of the hundreds of songs created by the Sons of the Pioneers, the most famous singing group in the history of Western music. Charter members Roy Rogers (Len Slye), Bob Nolan, Tim Spencer, and brothers Hugh and Karl Farr (two gifted instrumentalists from Texas) developed a

The Sons of the Pioneers
by
Bill O'Neal and Fred Goodwin

unique style of vocal control and harmony that became the group's trademark. During the 1930s and 1940s, the prolific Nolan, along with other members of the Pioneers, composed hundreds of new songs, primarily for film appearances. Although Roy Rogers left the group for movie stardom, the Pioneers appeared with "the King of the Cowboys" in forty-two films. There were one hundred movie appearances in all, including *Rio Grande* and *The Searchers* with John Wayne. Alumni of the Pioneers include Pat Brady, Lloyd Perryman, and Ken Curtis, among others. Today the Sons of the Pioneers carry on the long traditions of their group in Branson, Missouri.

The Sons of the Pioneers is a must for any fan of Western movies and music. Chapters include: "Reunion," "Founding Fathers," "On the Silver Screen," "With Charles Starrett," "Reunited with Roy," The Pioneers and World War II," "The Postwar Years," "The Pioneers in Transition," "Empty Saddles," and "Tumbling Along the Tumbleweed Trail."

- **Softcover**
- **250 pages**
- **Many, many photographs**
- **Complete filmography**
- **Complete listing of recordings and albums**

$26.95
(+ $3⁰⁰ shipping)

EMPIRE PUBLISHING, INC. • PO BOX 717 • MADISON, NC 27025

Other Fine Western Movie Books Available from Empire Publishing, Inc:

ABC's of Movie Cowboys by Edgar M. Wyatt. $5.00
Audie Murphy: Now Showing by Sue Gossett. $30.00
Back in the Saddle: Essays on Western Film and Television Actors edited by Garry Yoggy. $24.95.
Bill Elliott, The Peaceable Man by Bobby Copeland. $15.00.
Bob Steele, Stars and Support Players by Bob Nareau. $20.00
B-Western Actors Encyclopedia by Ted Holland. $30.00.
Buster Crabbe, A Self-Portrait as told to Karl Whitezel. $24.95.
B-Western Boot Hill: A Final Tribute to the Cowboys and Cowgirls Who Rode the Saturday Matinee Movie Range (revised edition) by Bobby Copeland. $15.00.
The Cowboy and the Kid by Jefferson Brim Crow, III. $5.90.
Duke, The Life and Image of John Wayne by Ronald L. Davis. $12.95.
The Films and Career of Audie Murphy by Sue Gossett. $18.00.
The Films of the Cisco Kid by Francis M. Nevins, Jr. $19.95.
The Films of Hopalong Cassidy by Francis M. Nevins, Jr. $19.95
From Pigskin to Saddle Leather: The Films of Johnny Mack Brown by John A. Rutherford. $19.95.
The Gene Autry Reference-Trivia-Scrapbook by David Rothel. $25.00.
The Golden Corral, A Roundup of Magnificent Western Films by Ed Andreychuk. $29.95.
The Hollywood Posse, The Story of a Gallant Band of Horsemen Who Made Movie History by Diana Serra Cary. $16.95.
Hoppy by Hank Williams. $29.95
In a Door, Into a Fight, Out a Door, Into a Chase, Movie-Making Remembered by the Guy at the Door by William Witney. $32.50.
John Ford, Hollywood's Old Master by Ronald L. Davis. $14.95.
John Wayne—Actor, Artist, Hero by Richard D. McGhee. $25.00.
John Wayne, An American Legend by Roger M. Crowley. $29.95.
Last of the Cowboy Heroes by Budd Boetticher. $32.50.
The Life and Films of Buck Jones, the Silent Era by Buck Rainey. $14.95.
The Life and Films of Buck Jones, the Sound Era by Buck Rainey. $24.95.
More Cowboy Movie Posters by Bruce Hershenson. $20.00.
More Cowboy Shooting Stars by John A. Rutherford and Richard B. Smith, III. $18.00.
The Official TV Western Roundup Book by Neil Summers and Roger M. Crowley. $34.95.
Quiet on the Set, Motion Picture History at the Iverson Movie Location Ranch by Robert G. Sherman. $14.95.
Randolph Scott, A Film Biography by Jefferson Brim Crow, III. $25.00.
Richard Boone: A Knight Without Armor in a Savage Land by David Rothel. $30.00.
Riding the (Silver Screen) Range, The Ultimate Western Movie Trivia Book by Ann Snuggs. $15.00.
Riding the Video Range, The Rise and Fall of the Western on Television by Garry A. Yoggy. $75.00.
The Round-Up, A Pictorial History of Western Movie and Television Stars Through the Years by Donald R. Key. $27.00.
Roy Rogers, A Biography, Radio History, Television Career Chronicle, Discography, Filmography, etc. by Robert W. Phillips. $65.00.
The Roy Rogers Reference-Trivia-Scrapbook by David Rothel. $25.00.
Saddle Gals, A Filmography of Female Players in B-Westerns of the Sound Era by Edgar M. Wyatt and Steve Turner. $10.00.
Saddle Pals: A Complete B-Western Roster of the Sound Era by Garv Towell and Wayne E. Keates. $5.00.
Singing in the Saddle by Douglas B. Green. $34.95.
The Sons of the Pioneers by Bill O'Neal and Fred Goodwin. $26.95.
Television Westerns Episode Guide by Harris M. Lentz, III. $95.00.
Tex Ritter: America's Most Beloved Cowboy by Bill O'Neal. $21.95.
They Still Call Me Junior by Frank "Junior" Coghlan. $37.50.
Those Wide Open Spaces by Hank Williams. $29.95.
Tim Holt by David Rothel. $30.00.
The Tom Mix Book by M. G. "Bud" Norris. $24.95.
Trail Talk, Candid Comments and Quotes by Performers and Participants of The Saturday Matinee Western Films by Bobby Copeland. $12.50.
The Western Films of Sunset Carson by Bob Carman and Dan Scapperotti. $20.00.
Western Movies: A TV and Video Guide to 4200 Genre Films compiled by Michael R. Pitts. $25.00.
Westerns Women by Boyd Magers and Michael G. Fitzgerald. $36.50.
Whatever Happened to Randolph Scott? by C. H. Scott. $12.95.
White Hats and Silver Spurs, Interviews with 24 Stars of Film and Television Westerns of the 1930s-1960s. $38.50.

Ask for our complete listing of 300+ movie books!

Add $3.00 shippping/handling for 1st book + $1.00 for each additional book.

Empire Publishing, Inc. • PO Box 717 • Madison, NC 27025-0717 • Ph 336-427-5850